0125201

Books are to be returned on or before
the last date below.

185278875'5'

The Spirit of Capitalism
and the Protestant Ethic

To the memory of Max and Marianne Weber

The Spirit of Capitalism and the Protestant Ethic

An Enquiry into the Weber Thesis

Michael H. Lessnoff

Department of Politics
University of Glasgow, UK

Edward Elgar

Published by

Edward Elgar Publishing Limited
Gower House
Croft Road
Aldershot
Hants GU11 3HR
England

Edward Elgar Publishing Company
Old Post Road
Brookfield
Vermont 05036
USA

British Library Cataloguing in Publication Data

Lessnoff, Michael H.
 Spirit of Capitalism and the Protestant
 Ethic: Enquiry into the Weber Thesis
 I. Title
 330.122

Library of Congress Cataloguing in Publication Data

Lessnoff, Michael H. (Michael Harry)
  The spirit of capitalism and the Protestant ethic : an enquiry
 into the Weber thesis / Michael H. Lessnoff.
  160p. 22cm.
 Includes bibliographical references and index.
  1. Weber, Max, 1864–1920. Protestantische Ethik under der Geist des
 Kapitalismus. 2. Capitalism—Religious aspects—Protestant
 churches. 3. Sociology, Christian. 4. Christian ethics.
 5. Calvinism. 6. Protestant work ethic. I. Title.
 BR115.E3W433 1944
 306.6—dc20

94–21837
CIP

ISBN 1 85278 875 5

Printed in Great Britain at the University Press, Cambridge

Contents

Acknowledgements   vii

1 What the Weber Thesis is, and what it is not   1

2 The pre-Reformation background   18

3 Weber's primary Protestant ethic: the work ethic   27

4 Weber's secondary Protestant ethic: the profit ethic   42

5 The Westminster Assembly's Shorter Catechism and   59
     its sources

6 The Spirit of Capitalism and the Protestant Ethic   86

7 Postscript on the modern world   105

Appendix A The Glasgow city motto – an epitome of   115
               the Weber Thesis?

Appendix B List of Protestant catechisms that discuss   120
               the Decalogue's commandment against
               stealing

Notes   124

General Bibliography   133

Index   141

Acknowledgements

I have incurred a number of debts of gratitude in the writing of this book. I am grateful to the Nuffield Foundation, whose financial support in the form of a Small Grant enabled me to carry out research in libraries in London, Oxford and Cambridge into catechisms of the sixteenth and seventeenth centuries. An article based on this research was published in the *Scottish Journal of Religious Studies*, and I should like to thank its editor for permission to make use of that material, as well as an earlier article, in the present book. I am grateful also to the *International Journal of Sociology and Social Policy* for permission to draw on an article published in that journal. I owe thanks to my colleagues Joe Houston, for help and advice on theological matters, and Mary Haight, who read through the entire book before publication. Last, but very far from least, my grateful thanks are due (once again) to Elspeth Shaw, Avril Johnstone and Eithne Johnstone, secretaries of the Glasgow University Politics Department, for preparing the text in camera-ready form, with remarkable skill and good humour.

1 What the Weber Thesis is, and what it is not

Max Weber's famous thesis, postulating a link between the Protestant Reformation (more accurately, 'ascetic Protestantism') and the rise of modern capitalism, has been so much discussed that it may be necessary to justify to the reader yet another enquiry into the subject. To my mind, the enormous importance of the question that Weber sought to answer, and the brilliance of his essay (not the same thing as its truth), are sufficient justification. Nor can it be said that the problem Weber set himself has been solved. But there is another, more melancholy justification, namely the fact that the general quality of argument on the Weber Thesis has been (despite some conspicuous exceptions) extremely low. It is therefore not so difficult as might be supposed, from the sheer volume of past discussion, to make a new and useful contribution to the subject. In fact, not a few of the discussants, especially critics of the Thesis, give the impression of not knowing what it is (for example, differences in teachings on usury play no part in Weber's argument). That is why this introductory chapter has the title that it has.

A SUMMARY OF THE WEBER THESIS

As a sociologist, Weber saw his life's work as nothing less than the comparative analysis of world civilizations. Above all, he was fascinated by the different historical trajectories traced by Western civilization, and the civilizations of the East. Why, in particular, was it Western civilization (Western Europe and North America) that gave birth, a few centuries ago, to that dramatic, unprecedented and qualitatively enormous transformation of human life and society known as the Industrial Revolution, with all that has flowed from it? It is, of course, obvious – and by Weber's time had become a commonplace – that the explanation must involve the economic system which was the vehicle of this Revolution, namely capitalism. But what exactly was it about this system that carried such revolutionary potential? And why did such a revolutionary economic system develop in the first place?

Weber's answers are given in his famous essay, *The Protestant Ethic and the Spirit of Capitalism* (though not there alone). Indeed, this title names the two entities which in his view provide the answers to these questions. This means that, initially at least, the Weber Thesis can be represented schematically as a causal chain involving four terms: the 'Protestant ethic' (PE), the 'spirit of capitalism' (SC), 'modern Western capitalism' (MWC) and the Industrial Revolution (IR). Thus (if arrows are used to represent cause-effect relations):

$$PE \longrightarrow SC \longrightarrow MWC \longrightarrow IR$$

All these terms, except the Industrial Revolution, require definition – the other three are coinages by Weber. Admittedly, it is difficult to provide completely separate definitions of 'modern Western capitalism' and the 'spirit of capitalism', since the former is in part a pattern of economic behaviour, the latter a set of ideas motivating and governing that behaviour (which however is also channelled by the structural elements of the capitalist system). Nevertheless, the attempt must be made, even at the cost of some repetition, for a behaviour pattern and a set of ideas, however mutually implicated they may be, remain different entities.

Modern Western capitalism

Modern Western capitalism, for Weber, is a peculiar form of acquisitive or gain-seeking enterprise, having the following features among others:

1. Gain is sought not by violent means such as war, but peacefully through trade ('the market'), that is by selling at a profit. Necessary inputs (notably labour services) are bought, not acquired by violence or legal coercion (Weber 1930, pp. 17, 21-2). Since trade is, in modern jargon, a positive-sum game, whereas war is a zero-sum game, the significance of this for economic development is obvious.

2. Gain is sought by legal and honest means only (Weber 1930, pp. 53-4, 56-7). Again, honest trading is a positive-sum transaction, swindling a zero-sum transaction. (Of course, Weber was not so naive as to suppose that dishonesty and swindling are absent from the capitalism of the modern West. However, his concept of

'modern Western capitalism', like all his theoretical concepts, is an 'ideal type', designed, in this case, to capture what he held to be both distinctive and significant in the phenomenon – here, the degree of its conformity to norms of legality and honesty.)
3. The gain-seeking enterprise is a distinct and continuing entity – the 'firm' – the running of which is a career. It is distinct from the family, and from the sporadic undertakings of adventurers and speculators (Weber 1930, pp. 20-2).
4. Gain-seeking is rationalized by orientation to the firm's balance-sheet, that is to 'calculations in terms of capital. Everything is done in terms of [money] balances', by means of which the profitableness of projects can be estimated in advance and recorded after the event (Weber 1930, p. 18). The firm's profits (revenues minus costs) can thus be, and are, measured with some precision.
5. Not only does the firm (or businessman) seek profit but (subject to the restraints detailed above at 1 and 2) as much profit as possible (Weber 1930, pp. 65-8). Such economic agents are not content to earn a 'traditional' level of income, but aim, one might say, at profit-maximization. (The significance of this for economic development is again evident; a profit-maximizer will be eager to adopt technical improvements, whereas a traditionalist will not.)

In summary: modern Western capitalism involves the unremitting devotion by businessmen to the pursuit of maximum money profit through non-violent, legal and honest means.

The spirit of capitalism

Modern Western capitalism includes both structural and behavioural elements, but Weber's focus is on the latter, for he found them to be, in both senses of the word, peculiar. In particular, the unremitting pursuit of maximum profit, of ever more profit, which might be mistaken for a simple expression of self-interest, is in fact nothing of the kind. It is peculiar both in the sense of being an unusual behaviour pattern specific to the modern Western bourgeois class, and in the sense that it bespeaks a strange, even unnatural elevation of a single economic end – pecuniary acquisition – above all others. Instead of pecuniary gain being seen as a means to ease and enjoyment, the latter are eschewed, since they would interfere with the maximization of profit. Profit maximization has become an end in itself. Why? Because, according to Weber, it has come to be seen as a duty, indeed the highest good, and the badge of virtue. This is the 'spirit of capitalism'. Weber calls it an *ethic* (Weber 1930, p. 51):

> the *summum bonum* of this ethic, the earning of more and more money, combined with the strict avoidance of all spontaneous enjoyment of life ... is thought of ... purely as an end in itself ... Man is dominated by the making of money, by acquisition as the ultimate purpose of his life. Economic acquisition is no longer subordinated to man as the means for the satisfaction of his material needs. This reversal of what we should call the natural relationship is ... definitely a leading principle of [modern] capitalism (Weber 1930, p. 53).

The 'spirit of capitalism', (which Weber, famously, found paradigmatically expressed in the writings of Benjamin Franklin) (Weber 1930, pp. 48-52, 64) may thus be called a 'profit ethic'. The ethic specifies both an *end*, and a number of *means* to that end. Both end and means are prescribed as duties. Among these means are such virtues as industry, frugality, punctuality, and honesty. But these elements of the spirit of capitalism are valued only because they are instrumental to the '*summum bonum*', the earning of more and more money. (Honesty here has an interestingly ambiguous status. It can be viewed as a *restraint* on gain-seeking, but also as, in the long run, a *means* to it – because, in the familiar cliché, 'honesty is the best policy'.) A final noteworthy element of this 'profit ethic' is that business success is seen as 'the result and expression of virtue' (Weber 1930, p. 54).

The Protestant ethic

The spirit of capitalism is a set of motivating ideas – a peculiar one, in Weber's view, and hence requiring explanation. His explanation is another set of ideas – the Protestant ethic. What exactly is the difference between these two sets of ideas? One difference is obvious. The bearers of the spirit of capitalism must be capitalists or, more broadly, economic agents operating in a capitalist system, whereas the proponents of the Protestant ethic must be men of religion – theologians, preachers, divines. But the Protestant ethic is nevertheless what Weber called a 'secular ethic', that is an ethic for this world, even if derived from more fundamental religious principles. As such, it includes, or yields, an economic ethic. One might therefore expect the Protestant ethic and the spirit of capitalism to be essentially identical in content, even although the relation between them postulated by Weber would amount to a religious influence on economic conduct. However, careful attention to Weber's argument reveals that this is *not* so. This is a fact of great importance, not least to the argument of this book.

To explain the point, it is necessary to summarize Weber's account of the historical development of Protestant doctrine in the sixteenth and seventeenth centuries. From the human standpoint, the most fundamental tenet of Protestantism is its salvation doctrine – salvation by faith alone (*sola fide*). Works have no salvific efficacy. Nevertheless, Protestantism does of course have a doctrine of works, that is of human behaviour that is pleasing to God and hence obligatory for men. Weber's 'Protestant ethic' results from the interaction, over time, of these two doctrines. It was first fully elaborated, he claims, within the Calvinist Reformed Churches (though not by Calvin himself). Nevertheless, both Luther and Calvin played an essential role.

Luther not only originated Protestant solifideism, he also decisively altered the Christian conception of good works, through his doctrine of the earthly calling (Weber 1930, pp. 79-81). The earthly calling is, in effect, every legitimate and useful social role, conceived as part of the divine order for men. To perform the duties of such a calling is to serve and love one's neighbour, as commanded by God – it is thus 'the only way to live acceptably to God' (Weber 1930, p. 81). All such callings, furthermore, are of equal worth in the sight of God. Conversely, withdrawal from the world, as by the medieval monk, is valueless from a religious point of view. The decisive innovation involved in this doctrine, says Weber, is that it views 'fulfilment of duties in worldly affairs as the highest form which the moral activity of the individual could assume' (Weber 1930, p. 80).

Calvin accepted Luther's doctrine of the calling, but it was, according to Weber, subtly yet crucially modified as a result of the characteristically Calvinist salvation doctrine, absolute double predestination (Weber 1930, pp. 98-127). This doctrine asserts that God has determined, by immutable decree at the beginning of time, to save certain human beings (the elect) through his divine grace, and to damn the rest (the reprobate) eternally, by withholding his grace from them. Salvation means eternal bliss in the presence of God, damnation means eternal torment in hell; but the distinction has nothing to do with any difference in merit between the saved and the damned: it results solely from God's power and will, which give some saving faith and deny it to others. Furthermore, Calvin held that the elect are a small minority (Weber 1930, p. 103). Although it has often been said that this doctrine became more central to Calvin's followers than it was to Calvin (and it did indeed, as confessional distinctions grew sharper, become the very badge of Calvinist theology), nevertheless Calvin himself described it (with some complacency) as 'terrifying' (McGrath 1990, p. 167). Weber agreed. It is terrifying above all because there appears to be no way in which the individual can affect his own fate, and no reliable way even of knowing what it is to be. Or rather, the only criterion is the 'subjective' (or inner) one of faith in Jesus Christ; there is no 'objective' criterion (Weber 1930, p. 110). On the face of it, there might seem to be no particular difficulty in subscribing to the necessary faith, and many certainly have professed it. But – if the elect are few – many or most professing Christians must be deceiving themselves, must lack 'true' Christian faith. The subjective criterion – the only criterion – appears fallible. Such a doctrine, says Weber, must have placed its adherents in a psychologically intolerable position: it could not therefore be long maintained in its full rigour. As Weber wrote:

> How was [Calvin's] doctrine borne in an age in which the after-life was not only more important, but in many ways also more certain, than all the interests of life in this world? The question, Am I one of the elect? must sooner or later have arisen for every believer ... And how can I be sure of this state of grace?... Quite naturally [Calvin's] attitude was impossible for his followers as early as Beza [Calvin's successor in Geneva], and above all, for the broad mass of ordinary men. For them the *certitudo salutis* in the sense of the recognizability of the state of grace became of absolutely predominant importance (Weber 1930, pp. 109-110).

The need, then, was for a reliable, objective sign of grace, or of true faith. According to Weber, Calvin's successors provided this in the most obvious way, namely by resort to 'good works'. Good works, 'a type of Christian conduct which served to increase the glory of God', became the sign of true faith (Weber 1930, p. 114). They became, not a means to salvation, but the means of getting rid of the fear of damnation. In this way, good works came, paradoxically, to have a pivotal position in Reformed Protestant psychology (Weber 1930, pp. 110-115).

It now becomes crucial, of course, how good works are defined. What is the type of Christian conduct which serves to increase the glory of God? An important part of the answer is punctual and conscientious fulfilment of the duties of one's earthly calling (Weber 1930, pp. 108-119). But there is more to it. Another aspect of the Calvinist secular morality is what may be called 'puritanism', that is the doctrine that the flesh must be 'mortified', and hence all self-indulgence, ease, worldly pleasure, luxury, self-aggrandizing display, and so on, must be avoided or at least minimized (Weber 1930, pp. 105, 121, 153-4, 167-9). Applied to the earthly calling, this yields (in the economic sphere) the famous 'work ethic' – the prescription of relentless and unremitting devotion to the performance of one's economic role in society. As Weber put it: 'in order to attain ... self-confidence intense worldly activity is recommended as the most suitable means. It and it alone disperses religious doubts and gives the certainty of grace' (Weber 1930, p. 112).

As expounded so far, the Protestant ethic has two elements, one positive and one negative. The positive element is the work ethic; the negative element is the anathema on self-indulgence. It is obvious that these elements correlate with elements of Weber's spirit of capitalism; the work ethic corresponds to the latter's virtue of industriousness, the proscription of self-indulgence to its virtue of frugality. Nor is it hard to see how businessmen or artisans, motivated by these elements of the Protestant ethic, would be more likely to achieve success and to make money (the proscription on self-indulgence, obviously, would reduce the diversion of profit into consumption, facilitating investment and hence further profit). Precisely this point is sometimes taken to be the essence of the Weber thesis. It is of great importance, however, to see that it is not. Weber's thesis is that the Protestant ethic generated, not merely economic success, but a new economic ethic, the spirit of capitalism. The spirit of capitalism, we saw, is a *profit* ethic. So far, we have seen no sign of a profit ethic in Weber's Protestant ethic, nor any religious rationale for one. In the spirit of capitalism, the virtues of industry and frugality are deemed to be such because they are means to maximize profit. In the Protestant ethic the duties to work and to abstain from self-indulgence have no such status. Simply, they are considered as forms of behaviour pleasing to God. As such, they are absolute imperatives.

But did the Protestant ethic include a profit ethic? According to Weber, it did – or rather, it generated one, what Weber calls 'the providential interpretation of profit-making' (Weber 1930, p. 163). This has two elements. The first is an alleged correlation between business success and divine grace. As Weber put it, it 'came to be of great importance for Puritanism that God would bless his own in this life ... – and also in the material sense' (Weber 1930, p. 164). Hence the 'stock remark about those good men who had successfully followed the divine hints – "God blesseth his trade" ' (Weber 1930, p. 163). The second element is the notion that pursuit of gain in business is a divine command – in effect, that there is a divine injunction to maximize profit (*Ibid.*; Weber 1930, p. 171). *A priori*, this seems to be an astonishing idea. Nevertheless, by the addition of a profit ethic consisting of these two elements, Weber has greatly increased the substantive similarity of the Protestant ethic and the spirit of capitalism, though he has not made them identical. The remaining, major difference is that, in the economic framework of the spirit of capitalism, the connection between profit-seeking on the one hand, and industry and frugality on the other, is simple and obvious, whereas in the religious framework of the Protestant ethic no such obvious connection exists.

In discussion of the Weber Thesis, the role played therein by a Protestant profit ethic has sometimes been overlooked, or even denied. In particular, some defenders of Weber are inclined to stress the point that, according to his Thesis, ascetic Protestantism boosted modern Western capitalism *unintentionally*. This may in a sense be true, but it can also mislead. In fact, Weber may himself have misled his readers on the point. In one part of *The Protestant Ethic and the Spirit of Capitalism* he warns them against the idea that 'any of the founders or representatives of [Calvinism, and the other Puritan sects]' saw 'the promotion of what we have called the spirit of capitalism' as 'in any sense the end of his life-work', or 'that the pursuit of worldly goods, conceived as an end in itself, was to any of them of any positive value'. Thus, he concludes, 'the cultural consequences of the Reformation were to a great extent, perhaps in its [economic] aspects predominantly, unforeseen and even unwished-for results of the labours of the reformers' (Weber 1930, pp. 89-90). This may be true of the 'founders', but cannot be *entirely* true of *all* the 'representatives': Weber's 'providential interpretation of profit-making' implies as much. Quite explicitly, according to his 'providential' interpretation, 'acquisition [of wealth], as a performance of duty in a calling, is not only morally permissible, but actually enjoined' (Weber 1930, p. 163). It is not in that case unforeseen or unwished-for, even if it is not an end in itself either. Such is Weber's 'Protestant profit ethic'. It is not identical to the profit ethic of the 'spirit of capitalism', but is crucial to Weber's explanation of its genesis.

I do not believe that Weber gave a satisfactory account of the Protestant profit ethic, and this will be a major focus of the present book. To put it another way, he does not show any logical connection, from a religious point of view, between the work ethic and the profit ethic. Indeed, he fails to give any theological explanation for the profit ethic (in marked contrast to his extended theological explanation of the work ethic). Instead, he simply illustrates his point by means of quotations, notably from Richard Baxter's *Christian Directory*. The key passage is as follows: 'If God shows you a way in which you may lawfully get more than in another way (without wrong to your soul or any other), if you refuse this, and choose the less gainful way, you cross one of the ends of your calling ...' (Weber 1930, p. 162) This is indeed a striking passage from a major spokesman of English Puritanism, but is none the less puzzling for that. Nor, obviously, can Weber make his case by means of one or a few quotations. How representative are they? There is also another problem. Baxter's *Christian Directory* was published in 1673, in other words at a rather late stage in the evolution of Protestantism. So, whether or not Baxter's teaching is representative, might it not be a response to the development of capitalism, rather than a cause of it? May its function not be what Marxists would call ideological?

Another consideration may strengthen such a suspicion. Weber himself argued that the Protestant ethic boosted capitalism, not only by creating 'modern' profit-maximizing capitalists, but also by providing them with a disciplined and motivated labour-force (Weber 1930, pp. 61-3, 177). The latter, of course, is the result of the work ethic. Clearly, workers thus motivated by the work ethic were not carriers of the spirit of capitalism. Or perhaps one might say that what we have here is a spirit of capitalism of a Marxist kind – a work ethic for the workers, a profit ethic for the capitalists. Be that as it may, the more general point is that work ethic and profit ethic do not necessarily coincide.

It therefore seems to me appropriate, in discussing the Weber Thesis, to *divide* his so-called Protestant ethic into two parts; roughly, the work ethic and the profit ethic. These I shall call, respectively, the primary Protestant ethic and the secondary Protestant ethic. (The ethic of puritanism is common to both, but this does not make them the same.) Let us now reconsider the schematic version of the Weber Thesis given at the start of this chapter: PE—>SC—>MWC—>IR. Thus stated, the Thesis makes three causal claims; but it also makes (obviously) four *existence* claims – the existence of the four causally linked phenomena. In principle all seven claims could be controverted; in practice, however, few people are likely to deny the reality of modern Western capitalism or the Industrial Revolution, or of the causal link between them. On the other hand, the very existence of Weber's Protestant ethic, and of his spirit of capitalism, are controversial, as is his assertion of a causal connection between them; likewise controversial is his claim that modern Western capitalism is the fruit of a special capitalist spirit. These controversies are the essence of the debate about the Weber Thesis, and all will be considered (certainly not settled) in this book. But quite crucial to the Weber Thesis, as I have suggested, is Weber's postulation of a profit ethic, both as part of his Protestant ethic, and as the *summum bonum* of his spirit of capitalism. If there was no (widespread) Protestant *profit* ethic, the notion of the spirit of capitalism as the offspring of the Protestant ethic is untenable; if there was no capitalist profit *ethic*, then Weber's spirit of capitalism would be non-existent, and obviously could not be the seed of modern Western capitalism. I shall not, however, confine myself to reviewing Weber's claims, but shall also explore other possible links between Protestantism and capitalism.

What the Weber Thesis is not

The scope of the present study of the Weber Thesis is, inevitably, limited (the precise nature of the limitation will be explained more fully below). Before doing this, however, it seems worthwhile to try to state more exactly what the scope of the Thesis itself is – and also what it is not. (Some of the points I am about to make may seem obvious, but they have not always been obvious to Weber's critics.)

Firstly, Weber (obviously?) did not claim that the Protestant ethic *alone* was enough to bring about the modern capitalist system. As he himself pointed out, numerous other structural factors were also necessary, or played a part – the development of money and markets, credit institutions, devices such as double-entry book-keeping, the rule of law, the separation of the family from the economic unit, and so on (Weber 1930, pp. 21-2, 25; Weber 1961, pp. 208, 250, 253). So what exactly was the contribution of the Protestant ethic? This question cannot be answered precisely, nor did Weber attempt to do so. At one extreme, Weber could be interpreted as claiming that, without ascetic Protestantism and its ethic, the development of Western capitalism to the point where it transformed society would not have occurred. A more moderate interpretation is that the Protestant ethic significantly helped (and speeded up) that development. Weber is, I think, committed to at least the latter thesis.

But Weber is certainly not committed to the (absurd) proposition that without the Protestant ethic capitalism is impossible. As he himself pointed out, capitalism has existed in all civilizations, East and West, before as well as after the Protestant Reformation (Weber 1930, p. 19). However, Weber was struck by the fact that only in the West, and after the Reformation, did it develop in a way, and on a scale, sufficient to bring about an Industrial Revolution and an industrial civilization. It therefore seems a not implausible hypothesis that there was something special about this post-Reformation Western capitalism. Weber's contention is that the special factor was contributed by 'ascetic Protestantism'.

However, Weber's Thesis, that religion can decisively influence economics, does not in the least entail a denial that causation may work the other way. Weber's views on this matter are stated in his *Sociology of Religion*:

> the middle class, by virtue of its distinctive pattern of economic life, inclines in the direction of a rational ethical religion, *wherever conditions are present for the emergence of a rational ethical religion* [emphases added]. When one compares the life of ... the urban artisan or the small trader, with the life of the peasant, it is clear that middle-class life has far less connection with nature. Consequently, dependence on magic for influencing the irrational forces of nature cannot play the same role for the urban dweller as for the farmer ... The economic foundation of the urban man's life has a far more rational essential character, viz. calculability and capacity for purposive manipulation. Furthermore, the artisan and in certain circumstances even the merchant lead economic existences which influence them to entertain the view that honesty is the best policy, that fruitful work and the performance of obligations will find their reward and are "deserving" of just compensation. For these reasons, small traders and artisans are disposed to accept a rational world view incorporating an ethic of compensation ... The peasants, on the other hand, are much more remote from this notion of compensation ... The belief in ethical compensation is even more alien to warriors and financial magnates who have economic interests in war (Weber 1965-6, p. 97).

Here, Weber clearly acknowledges the propensity of middle-class strata to adhere to an 'ethical' religion. Obviously such a religion is favoured if these strata are numerous and influential. But, Weber goes on, it is not created by them, but by 'prophets and reformers'. 'Only a congregational religion, especially one of the rational and ethical type, could ... win followers easily, particularly among the urban lower middle classes; and then, given certain circumstances, *exert a lasting influence on the pattern of life of these classes. This is what actually happened*' (Weber 1965-6, pp. 98-9, emphases added). It is hard not to believe that Weber, in these last words, had 'ascetic Protestantism' in mind. Its teachings, in other words, were of a sort to attract middle-class (bourgeois) adherents, because of its congruence with their experience and values. Nevertheless, it significantly altered their mode of life – as asserted by the Weber Thesis.

From this follows another important point about what the Weber Thesis is not. It does not assert, or entail, that the Protestant ethic was something utterly new or unprecedented. For example, the notion that hard work and reliability are virtues is, as Weber implies in the passage just cited, one that is likely to arise in urban, middle-class strata without any help from religion. Thus, he was happy to concede that the work ethic was not an invention of 'ascetic Protestantism'. Nevertheless, in Weber's view, there was and there had to be something special about the *Protestant* work ethic. There had to be, because in the pre-modern era (and in the Eastern civilizations), any work ethic there may have been played a minor, subordinate role, for both social and ideological reasons. The dominant social and political stratum of medieval Europe was a warrior nobility or feudal aristocracy, which prized military virtues, lavish generosity and display, and despised the middle class and its ethic (Weber 1965-6, pp. 85, 88). Pre-Reformation European Christianity (Roman Catholicism as it is now called), the other great social and ideological force of the period, valued worldly life much less than monastic withdrawal from the world (Weber 1930, pp. 120-121). And, according to Weber, even the pre-Reformation work ethic was crucially different from the version introduced by ascetic Protestantism. In a non-religious context, work is naturally seen as an *instrumental* virtue – it is (for most men) necessary but unpleasant, necessary to enable them to survive, or to enjoy a pleasant, comfortable life. The Protestant work ethic is quite different. Work – diligence in an earthly calling – is a religious imperative, irrespective of mundane ends. It is required of all men, no matter how wealthy they are or become. It is a duty that never ends, except with physical decrepitude or death. This is the crucial difference.

More needs to be said about the relation between the Protestant ethic and pre-Reformation Christianity. It would be extremely surprising if there were no ideological continuity between the two, nor did Weber assert any such implausibility. On the contrary, he always treated Protestantism as a development within the tradition of Western civilization, that is, Judaeo-Christian civilization. Thus, in his great book on *Ancient Judaism*, he was at pains to seek out features of the Hebrew religion that foreshadowed, not only Christianity, but Protestantism and modern Western civilization more generally (among these features, he believed, were an unusual hostility to magic and emphasis on moral law) (Weber 1952, pp. 222, 245, 235-6; Weber 1961, p. 264). But whereas ancient Judaism was a tribal/national religion, Christianity was in principle universal. A highly significant consequence of this was that it broke with what Weber calls the double standard, which Judaism shared with all particularistic religions; that is, an absolute moral distinction between fellow-members of the community and outsiders. The former are to be treated with generosity, like brothers, while it is legitimate to deal with the latter quite amorally (Weber 1965-6, pp. 250-1). A universalistic religion and ethic, by contrast, treats all alike by the same ethical rules and is, in Weber's view, an indispensable condition of the development of modern Western civilization (Weber 1958, pp. 99-100). Also, in this and other ways, Christianity, as a universalistic religion, crucially undermined the strength of familial ties and obligations (which it rated as of little importance compared to the universalistic religious obligations) and thus facilitated the separation of family and economy that Weber considered an important contributory factor in the growth of modern Western capitalism. Last but not least is the role of pre-Reformation Christian monasticism as a precursor and even source of the Protestant ethic. As Weber wrote:

> [Christian asceticism] has had a definitely rational character in its highest Occidental forms as early as the Middle Ages, and ... even in antiquity. The great historical significance of Western monasticism, as contrasted with that of the Orient is based on this fact ... It had developed a systematic method of rational conduct [in order] to free man from the power of irrational impulses and his dependence on the world and on nature. It attempted to ... bring his actions under constant self-control with a careful consideration of their ethical consequences. Thus it trained the monk, objectively, as a worker in the service of the kingdom of God, and thereby further, subjectively, assured the salvation of his soul. This active self-control ... was also the most important practical ideal of Puritanism (Weber 1930, pp. 118-119).

However, he continued:

> On the other hand, the difference of the Calvinistic from the medieval asceticism is evident. It consisted in ... the transformation of asceticism to activity within the world ... [Also], in the course of its development Calvinism added ... the idea of the necessity of proving one's faith in worldly activity (Weber 1930, pp. 120-121).

More will be said in a later chapter about *doctrinal* parallels between the Protestant ethic and pre-Reformation monasticism.

A final, very important point about what the Weber Thesis is not, is the following. It is not, or rather not simply, a claim that the propagation of a certain set of ideas led to (or encouraged) a socio-economic transformation. That, indeed is part of it. Anyone who encountered, and accepted, the doctrines of ascetic Protestantism had a reason to act in accordance with them. However, as the philosopher Donald Davidson pointed out in a classic article, people do not always act on reasons they have for acting – probably we are moved to action by only a relatively small proportion of the reasons we entertain. Put another way, not all reasons for action cause action (Davidson 1980, pp. 3-19). A central theme of the Weber Thesis is to explain why the Protestant ethic could be a powerful motivator of action, not just for a few people but for large numbers. That it was a *religious* doctrine, accepted by many in an age of faith, is an important part of the explanation. More specifically, what Weber emphasized most was the explicit connection made by the Protestant ethic between a certain way of behaving in the world, and the fate of the individual's eternal soul – eternal bliss versus eternal torment. The Weber Thesis is as much (or more) a thesis about human psychology as about the filiation of ideas.

This gives rise to another important, and connected point, namely the importance or otherwise of the doctrine of predestination in its full Calvinist form (absolute double predestination) to Weber's Thesis. In my opinion, its importance has often been exaggerated in discussions of the Thesis. Weber's argument, as I interpret it, is that, historically, 'ascetic Protestantism' was a development from the strict doctrine of predestination, but that the latter was logically neither sufficient nor necessary for that development. As Weber remarks, the strictly logical implication of the doctrine is fatalism, not this-worldly activism (Weber 1930, p. 232) – so the doctrine of predestination cannot be in itself sufficient to generate the Protestant ethic. Nor is it necessary, for not only the Calvinist Churches were bearers of this ethic, according to Weber, but also other 'ascetic Protestant' groups which rejected the strict Calvinistic doctrine of predestination, notably Wesleyan Methodism and the Quakers (Weber 1930, pp. 139 ff., 148). What is vital, I suggest, is not predestination as such, but the connection postulated between certain sorts of this-worldly activity and the salvation of the soul. It is thus not a valid objection to Weber's argument that Richard Baxter, whom he quotes so copiously and relies on so heavily, was not a strictly orthodox Calvinist on the issue of predestination. Baxter, in fact has been described (inaccurately, as it happens) as a 'Puritan Arminian' (Spurr 1991, p. 314), and the same description can be (correctly) applied to John Wesley and his followers.[1] In both cases, what matters is the Puritanism, not the Arminianism. However, it will be worthwhile at this point to give some attention to Arminian and some other Protestant teachings on the subject of predestination.

Calvinism, Arminianism and Anglicanism

Jacob Arminius (1559-1609) was a theologian and minister of the Dutch Reformed Church who challenged its Calvinistic orthodoxy and was in due course condemned by it. (His followers were expelled and set up a rival church.) Orthodox Calvinism taught the utter sinfulness of human nature (since the Fall) and men's total incapacity to merit salvation. In justice, all deserve damnation. God is just to most, but merciful to a few, to whom only, by the power of his irresistible grace, he gives true faith. The former he has predestinated to eternal damnation, the latter to eternal salvation.

To Arminius, this doctrine was unacceptable because it seemed to him to make God the author of sin, yet to punish man for that sin. His teaching, therefore, is as follows. Man's nature is not totally sinful. God's grace is not offered only to the elect, nor is it irresistible. Men have freedom to accept or reject it. God, however, in his omniscience, has foreknowledge of which individuals will thus accept or reject his grace. Knowing this, he predestines the former to eternal salvation, the latter to eternal damnation. Arminius did not disagree with Calvin that the saved are few (Bangs 1971, pp. 350-5; Weir 1990, p. 20; White 1992, pp. 26, 30-1).

It seems to me clear that this doctrine is just as apt as the Calvinist one to create anxiety about salvation among its adherents, and just as apt to generate the view of life called by Weber the Protestant ethic. Though different from Calvin's, it is still a doctrine of predestination, and one that – logically – places a greater burden of responsibility on the individual for his own salvation. And yet the saved are few. There is absolutely nothing paradoxical about Arminian Puritanism.

In the late sixteenth and seventeenth centuries Arminianism attracted a following in the Church of England, and the Civil War of the mid-seventeenth century has sometimes been described as, at least in part, a struggle between Arminians and Puritans. Some historians believe that, in this struggle, not only were the Arminians the innovators theologically speaking, but that the Anglican orthodoxy that they challenged was a fully Calvinist one (Tyacke 1987, pp. viii, 1-3, 7, 245-6). Not all historians agree. Some point out that the Thirty-Nine Articles – the official Anglican confession of faith adopted in 1571 – differ from strict Calvinism in that they speak of predestination to salvation only, not to damnation. However, it is hard to see why this is considered (by some) to be a significant distinction. The Articles attribute salvation to God's will and grace alone. It follows logically that those not predestined to salvation are bound (in effect, predestined) to be damned. As the Articles themselves remark, the 'sentence of God's predestination' is likely to induce desperation in 'carnal persons, lacking the Spirit of Christ'.

The argument between Arminians and strict Calvinists arose, of course, out of the problem of reconciling God's omnipotence, God's justice, and men's sinfulness. Richard Baxter (so prominent in the Weber Thesis) responded to this problem by adopting a stance sometimes called Semi-Arminianism (Harrison 1937, p. 161), but better described as a compromise between Arminianism and Calvinism: that the saved are predestined by God's grace alone, whereas the rest (the reprobate) are left free, though their unbelief and impenitence are foreseen by God (Harrison 1937, p. 111). That this compromise is logically incoherent does not diminish by one whit Baxter's importance as a preacher of ascetic Protestantism. One can go further – the details of a theology of predestination are unimportant by comparison with the practical salvation ethic preached by this or that church or divine. Indeed this point was frequently made at the time (somewhat despairingly, one feels) by divines and others whose interests were more pastoral than theological – fine scholastic distinctions and disputes, they pleaded, should be kept within the ivory towers, and not allowed out to puzzle and disconcert the ordinary Christian (Spurr 1991, p. 316; White 1992, pp. 235, 300).[2]

Salvation doctrines of Protestantism and Roman Catholicism

Officially, the Protestant churches believed in salvation by faith alone, the Roman Catholics in salvation by faith and works. Yet paradoxically, according to Weber, 'ascetic Protestantism' produced a much more activist salvation ethic. Exposition of the Weber Thesis is not complete without a fuller account of this paradox. Here we come to an important *negative* side of the Protestant ethic, the means to salvation that it denied. Whatever secular morality the Roman church may have prescribed, and whatever the links postulated between it and salvation, its efficacy was undermined, Weber argues, by other doctrines on salvation taught by the old church. Weber stressed particularly the cycle of confession, penance and absolution – the priestly power to absolve from sin, and through confession and penance restore the sinner to a state of grace (Weber 1930, pp. 106, 116-7). The cycle could in principle be repeated endlessly. Other doctrines could be cited, similar in effect. For example, the medieval church, dubious about the possibility that a life in the secular world could be pleasing to God, accorded a special role to the monks who lived withdrawn from the world. Not only was their way of life the one best calculated to ensure their own salvation, it was also held that their prayers and holiness could be effectual in securing salvation for the rest of the Christian community (Lawrence 1984, pp. 62-3, 87-8). The concept of Purgatory brought further complications. A large array of devices was introduced by which the soul's sojourn in Purgatory could be shortened, and its attainment of salvation hastened – masses for the souls of the dead (wealthy men often left bequests to finance masses for their souls), prayers seeking the intercession of the saints on behalf of a departed person, the purchase of indulgences (the issue, of course, which sparked off the Reformation) (Lawrence 1984, p. 62; Weber 1930, p. 120). Also relevant is the particular conception of good works. Pre-Reformation Catholicism placed large importance on the saving merit of rituals of various kinds – according to the historian Christopher Hill, 'telling of beads, saying of paternosters, giving of candles, ... pilgrimages' etc. (Hill 1961, pp. 16-17). Ascetic Protestantism repudiated all of this as 'superstition', and correspondingly emphasized its conception of ethical behaviour.

Scope and limits of this book

It follows from what has been said above that, even if one could find every element of the Protestant ethic paralleled in Catholic teachings, the Weber Thesis would not thereby be destroyed, or even, necessarily, severely damaged.[3] Nor, on the other hand, is the Thesis established simply by showing that the Protestant ethic existed in exactly the form described by Weber. It would also be necessary to show that it *motivated* men in the way he claimed. That, however, would be a tall order, and is beyond the scope of this book (I have neither the necessary historical nor psychological knowledge). However, the Weber Thesis cannot be true *unless* the Protestant ethic, and the spirit of capitalism, both existed in the form asserted by Weber. These are among the questions that this book seeks to address.

2   The pre-Reformation background

In the previous chapter, I argued that a major problem besetting the Weber Thesis is that Weber's concept of the Protestant ethic is actually a dual concept – the work ethic and the profit ethic – and that the logical and theological connection between the two is unclear. I noted also the fact – acknowledged by Weber – that his so-called Protestant ethic was not without ideological precursors in the history of pre-Reformation Christendom. I shall now turn to the latter point in an attempt to throw some light on the former (which is, as I have stressed, a major focus of this book). In other words, I shall consider pre-Reformation Christian teachings on attitudes to work and to the acquisition of worldly wealth. We shall see that they were very different. It is not hard to find a pre-Reformation Christian work ethic of a sort; but nothing like a profit ethic in Weber's sense appears to be present. There will be two foci of attention, namely, the Western monastic tradition, and the attitude of Christian thinkers to economic life, especially that of the merchant. We shall see, also, that there is a bridge between the two, provided by the mendicant orders of the later Middle Ages.

Weber recognized that the 'inner-worldly asceticism' (*innerweltliche Askese*) of the Protestant ethic was, in some respects, a transposition into secular life of Western monastic asceticism. He cites with approval the insight of Sebastian Franck, who 'saw the significance of the Reformation in the fact that now every Christian had to be a monk all his life' (Weber 1930, p. 121). But what exactly does this mean? Among other things, it refers to the work ethic. 'Labour', Weber remarks, has always been 'an approved ascetic technique ... in the Western Church, in sharp contrast ... to the Orient' (Weber 1930, p. 158). There is no doubt that this is so, and that the roots of this Christian attitude to work run very deep. According to the Biblical story, mankind's need to work for a living is a consequence of the Fall and the resulting expulsion from Paradise, of Adam's sin and the inherited sinfulness of the human race. Work thus seems to have a two-fold significance: it is a necessity for post-lapsarian survival, but at the same time a punishment for and expiation of sin, and hence meritorious, or even obligatory, as a mortification of the flesh. It is worthwhile to trace the history, and consequences, of these ideas.

It seems that the Christian work ethic can be traced back to the very earliest monastic foundations, in the deserts of Egypt, Syria and Palestine, and even earlier, to the way of life of those men who were (in many respects) their inspiration, the desert hermits. From the very beginning (in the third and fourth centuries), the regimen of the desert hermits and monks included the requirement to work, both to support themselves, and as a means of warding off temptations (Lawrence 1984, pp. 5-6). Similar themes are repeated in the teachings of St Basil of Caesarea, an early (fourth century) and highly influential figure in the development of Christian monasticism: he stressed the virtue of work, as 'a means of perfecting the soul as well as supporting the community and providing for the poor' (Lawrence 1984, pp. 9-10). John Cassian, who founded monasteries at Marseilles in the early fifth century, again stressed at length, in his influential treatise on the monastic life, *De Institutis Coenobiorum*, the virtues of manual labour (Wenzel 1960 & 1967, pp. 18-19). Most significant of all, perhaps, is the famous Rule of St Benedict, the organizational basis of the Benedictine monasteries that spread all over Western Europe from the sixth century, thereby propagating ideas that had originated in the ascetic communities of the Egyptian desert. The emphasis placed by Benedict on labour is well known: for both economic and ascetic reasons, he prescribed for his monks some seven hours per day of manual work (compared with about three hours for reading). No provision was made for leisure, on the grounds (drawn from the Book of Proverbs) that 'idleness is the enemy of the soul' (Lawrence 1984, p. 30).

Equally instructive are the Benedictine rules on the acquisition of wealth. All possession of personal property by individual monks was, for ascetic reasons, forbidden; on the other hand, no such ban applied to the monastery as a corporate entity. This turned out to be the Achilles heel of Benedict's Rule: with the success of the Benedictine movement the monasteries became enormously wealthy, largely through gifts and bequests of laymen presumably interested in the salvation of their souls, both through their own munificence and by the efficacious prayers of the grateful monks. The poverty of the monks became much more nominal than real. Much time had to be devoted to administration of their estates, as well as prayers for the souls of benefactors and a greatly expanded and elaborated liturgy. Very little time was left for the manual work that had been so important to St Benedict. The material splendour attending the lives of monastic leaders, and the comfortable and often magnificent surroundings enjoyed by the rank and file became, in the eyes of many, a scandal (Lawrence 1984, pp. 61-3, 71; Little 1978, pp. 66-9).

Not surprisingly, therefore, there were many movements for the reformation of the Church and in particular of the monastic life before the Reformation. Most celebrated, most important and most relevant to the Weber Thesis are the Cistercians. The famous 'New Monastery' of Cîteaux was established in 1098, and its programme was the re-establishment of the strict Benedictine rule, with (*inter alia*) labour restored to its original pre-eminent role. Indeed, the asceticism of the Cistercians went further than that of Benedict, in theory at least, since it enjoined not only individual but corporate poverty. Gifts and bequests of land and other economic assets were rejected by the reformers – the Cistercians were to support themselves by their own efforts and their own hands. Such was the original intention. The unintended and ironic consequence of zealous Cistercian asceticism, as the movement spread widely throughout Western Europe, is well known. Their abbeys came to be among the most important economic producers of the High Middle Ages and, through their leaders' gifts of rational organization, immensely successful and immensely wealthy. This may seem like the story of the Benedictines all over again, but in fact there are crucial differences. The earlier Benedictine wealth had been based on gifts and bequests from laymen, and Benedictine estates were worked on the same basis as lay estates of the feudal era, by peasants who were tenants or serfs of their (monastic) feudal superior. By the time of the Cistercian ascendancy, the European economy had become to a much greater degree a market economy, and in this and other respects Cistercian economic organization and success seem almost like a slightly uncanny prefiguring of capitalism itself. The success and expansion of the Cistercian abbeys quite quickly meant that the labour of the monks themselves was insufficient. The solution adopted was the large-scale employment of the famous *conversi*, or lay brothers. The *conversus* was a semi-monk, but one chiefly occupied with performing the manual work required on the abbey estates. 'Recruited from the peasantry, they provided the permanent work-force of the monastery, leaving the choir monks the necessary leisure for liturgical and private prayer and reading' – and, of course, administration of the abbey's affairs, both religious and economic. In most Cistercian abbeys the *conversi* were the majority of the community. Seen in a purely economic light, the Cistercians had invented a two-class system, of administrators and labourers, and one which was brilliantly successful (Lawrence 1984, pp. 146-51, 161-3; Little 1978, pp. 90-6).

This story is fascinating in itself, but what interests us now is its relevance to the Weber Thesis. At first glance it may seem to support it (as Weber himself believed): in what looks almost like a trial run for the development of capitalism out of ascetic Protestantism, we see spectacular economic success developing out of ascetic Cistercian monasticism.[1] In a general sense this is accurate enough. However, as I have stressed, there is more to the Weber Thesis than the above proposition. In particular, his 'Protestant ethic' is dual, incorporating both a work ethic and a profit ethic. In the asceticism of the Cistercians we have seen how important was their version of the work ethic, but (while we see plenty of profits) we do not see a profit *ethic*. Weber may have thought otherwise: in one place he asserts that 'the economic prosperity of the monasteries was almost always considered a consequence of God's blessing' (Weber 1978, p. 1121), but without giving any further details. This assertion is dubious, at least so far as the Cistercians are concerned. Though welcome enough in obvious respects, economic prosperity was, from the strictly religious point of view, an embarrassment for a movement founded on a dedication not only to individual but to corporate poverty. Even if Weber is right, to say that wealth is God's blessing is not to say that it is a sign of virtue or salvation, still less that its maximization (by honest means) is a religious duty. In fact, many Cistercians saw economic success as a religious problem, even a disaster. As Caesarius of Heisterbach put it early in the thirteenth century: '[Monastic] discipline creates wealth, and wealth destroys the discipline' – this he called a 'tragic law'.[2] It is, indeed, obvious that wealth is a danger from the standpoint of ascetic ideals. Oddly enough, perhaps, Weber was fully aware of this point, and even stressed it in his discussion of ascetic Protestantism (Weber 1930, pp. 156-7, 174).[3] But he did not, in my judgment, sufficiently appreciate the questions this raises for his argument. He did not, that is, see how problematic is the incorporation into an ascetic ideal, in a logical or plausible way, of a profit ethic – as distinct from a work ethic. Our survey of medieval monasticism enables us to note once again the disjunction between the two – a work ethic is to be found therein, while a profit ethic is not.

The corruption, as many saw it, of Benedictine and Cistercian ideals led, in the later Middle Ages, to new solutions to the problem of the Christian life. Of these the most important were the mendicant orders, the Dominicans and Franciscans. Significantly, their conception of holiness did not call for life-long seclusion from the world in a monastery or friary, but rather required of the friar a life largely devoted to wandering and preaching in and to the world, dependent for his livelihood on the alms of the faithful. They thus became the quintessential exponents of later pre-Reformation Christian attitudes to secular economic activity.

Nobody, obviously, could deny the necessity of such activity: equally obviously, it was possible, from a Christian standpoint, to discriminate in the evaluation of different forms of economic life. We have already seen, in a monastic context, the relatively high Christian evaluation of labour, and low valuation (in theory at least) of the pursuit and acquisition of wealth. Much the same applies to the secular world. Because of God's curse on Adam, work was a necessity for human livelihood. Moderate wealth gained through work, therefore, was acceptable. But immoderate wealth, or wealth gained without work, was another matter. One reason for the condemnation of usury, for example, was that usurious gains are extracted without any work given in return, and are thus even a form of theft. 'The usurer wants to make a profit without doing any work, even while he is sleeping, which goes against the precepts of the Lord, who said, "By the sweat of your face shall you get bread to eat" ', wrote Thomas of Chobham in the thirteenth century (Le Goff 1988, p. 42).

In the earlier Middle Ages, the religious attitude to the merchant was almost as hostile as to the usurer. According to the early twelfth century theologian, Honorius of Autun, those who till the soil may hope for salvation, because they live simply and feed the people of God by the sweat of their brows; but the probability that a merchant can be saved is very slight, because his gains are overwhelmingly the result of fraud and avarice (Little 1978, p. 38). This was not an isolated opinion. Canon law consistently stated that it is difficult to avoid sin in the business of buying and selling, hence that 'A merchant is rarely or never able to please God'.

Weber, not surprisingly, laid great emphasis on these facts in arguing for his Thesis (Weber 1930, p. 73). However, he is open to some criticism for failing to acknowledge the degree to which these negative attitudes to the merchant had already changed before the Reformation. To a large degree, this change was due to the mendicant orders, the Dominicans and Franciscans. This may seem paradoxical, in view of the fact that the friars themselves were sworn to absolute poverty, and had to live by begging. More to the point, however, is that they saw their mission as preaching the Gospel to urban society. Whereas the Benedictines and Cistercians had taught that the world is utterly sinful, so that assurance of salvation can be achieved only by the monk who withdraws from it (and the layman's best hope also is through the monk's prayers), the message of the friars was that holiness and salvation could be achieved by Christian behaviour in the secular world – hence the famous Franciscan 'Third Order', consisting of confraternities of lay people sworn to holy living (Lawrence 1984, pp. 78, 87-8, 154, 192, 207-12, 216).

Apart from the fact that they promoted a generalized lay asceticism, these confraternities and their activities have little direct relevance to the Weber Thesis, but they are symptomatic of a changed attitude to secular economic life, including the activities of the merchant. The great Dominican theologians Albertus Magnus and Thomas Aquinas (drawing upon Aristotle) acknowledged the useful social function that the merchant performs – he is not simply a profiteer who sells goods for more than he pays for them (Little 1978, pp. 178-9).[4] His gains, therefore are not (or not necessarily) the result of fraud, but can be seen as payment for useful work. The merchant, if he is honest and contents himself with moderate gain, can therefore be a good Christian.

It would be a mistake to suppose that the ideas of scholastics such as Albert and Thomas could be influential only among an intellectual elite. These two thinkers, like many of their contemporaries, were not scholars only, but also belonged to one of the two great mendicant orders, which were dedicated to the evangelization of the common people, and numbered among their ranks many famous and passionate preachers (Little 1978, pp. 173-6; 186-8 *et seq.*). One of the most popular of these, the thirteenth century Franciscan Berthold of Regensburg, is also of interest in relation to the Weber Thesis. However, he needs to be interpreted with more care than has always been the case. Berthold is the author of a sermon called '*Von den Fünf Pfunden*', literally 'Of the Five Pounds', which is an application of the parable of the talents. The five pounds or talents are given by God to man to be used in His service. According to a recent discussion of Berthold's sermon (as translated into English), these talents or 'pounds' include one's body or person, one's life-span or time in the world, one's earthly goods, and one's calling or 'vocation, to which God, who has given every man his service, has predestined you'. Among these God-given vocations are those of the monk, the ploughman *and* the merchant – in fact all useful social functions (not including usury, however). It seems that Berthold here anticipates the idea of the earthly calling, which plays such an important role in Weber's concept of the Protestant ethic. Also, something like a Weberian work ethic can, it would seem, be deduced from Berthold's concept of vocation together with his view of time, which must never be wasted, but rather, he says, devoted to our proper tasks (Gurevich 1990, pp. 253-6).

Is the Weber Thesis damaged by this apparent pre-Reformation prefiguring of the 'primary Protestant ethic'? Weber, who was fully aware of Berthold of Regensburg and his activity (Weber 1930, p. 208), did not think so, and there are several reasons to believe that he was right. In the first place, the account of Berthold cited above is quite misleading. In fact, Berthold's sermon (printed in Vienna in 1862), never uses the term 'calling' or 'vocation' – in German, *Beruf*. Instead, he refers to the 'pound' (or 'talent') in question by the word *Amt*, which means 'office' or 'employment' (Berthold von Regensburg 1862, p. 13). To be sure, the religious importance attached by Berthold to work in the world is significant, especially in regard to the merchant: but the connotations of the terms *Beruf* and *Amt* are quite different. Weber admitted that a secular work ethic is to be found in Berthold's preaching: on the other hand, as he pointed out, worldly tasks continued to be seen, up to the Reformation, as constituting a way of life inferior to that of the monk (Berthold says as much explicitly) (Gurevich 1990, p. 254). And Weber further argued that the effects of any pre-Reformation religiously based inner-worldly asceticism were liable to be dissipated by the continuing availability of the confessional with attendant atonement through penance (Weber 1978, pp. 1113-14), not to mention vicarious merit, indulgences etc. In sum, Berthold's teachings demonstrate not that an equivalent of the Protestant work ethic already existed in the Middle Ages, but that that ethic is a development of an earlier tradition. On the other hand, it is worth noting that despite Berthold's acceptance of the merchant's social function, he did not subscribe to any profit ethic. On the contrary, he continually condemned avidity for wealth (Gurevich 1990, pp. 251, 254). His acceptance of the mercantile role, of a life devoted to buying and selling, is, naturally, conditional – not only on honest dealing, but on avoidance of the sin of avarice.

For avarice was not only a sin, but a deadly sin – one of the seven deadly (that is, damnable) sins which played such a dominant role in pre-Reformation Christian moralising. So also, of course, was sloth. Part of the relevant context for assessing the Weber Thesis, therefore, in particular the relation between the two elements of Weber's 'Protestant ethic', is the handling of these two sins by Christian thinkers in the medieval period. There seems to be little doubt that, so far as secular life is concerned, the sin of avarice was considered much the more important – and therefore, the more dangerous.

According to one authority avarice was, from the eleventh century, considered to be (along with pride) the pre-eminent vice, of clerics and laymen alike, as indicated by such statements as 'Avarice is the root of all evil' (Peter Damian), or 'There is no worse vice than avarice' (John of Salisbury) (Little 1978, p. 36). By contrast with such forthright and unequivocal condemnation of avarice, the concept of sloth was more complex, and (from a modern viewpoint) even anomalous. This requires some explanation.

The standard list of seven deadly sins grew out of a list of seven 'chief vices' proclaimed by Pope Gregory the Great in the sixth century (Wenzel 1960 & 1967, pp. 23, 28). Gregory's list includes all the sins of the standard list, except sloth. By the twelfth century, however, the list included, if not sloth exactly, the sin whose name came, a century or so later, to be translated by that term – namely *acedia* or *accidia*. The sin (or problem, or demon) of *acedia* had, however, a long history. It first became a focus of attention among the desert monks of Egypt, who used the term to refer to a state of listlessness and apathy (called by Evagrius Ponticus 'the noonday demon') which distracted the monk from his spiritual duties and even threatened his entire vocation (Wenzel 1960 & 1967, pp. 5, 10). Two points are of special interest: firstly, this *acedia* is a sin or temptation of monks, leading to failure to discharge the monks' spiritual duties. Secondly, Evagrius and many others recommended physical labour as a remedy for acedia. By the time *acedia* took its place among the seven deadly sins, it had become generalized to mean non-performance, or slack performance, of spiritual duties by all Christians, and also to include slackness or idleness of a more secular kind (Wenzel 1960 & 1967, pp. 31-7). What is of particular interest is the relative weight attached to these two elements. According to Siegfrid Wenzel, even at the end of the Middle Ages, 'Despite the treatise-writers' tendencies to comprehensiveness and to equate sloth with idleness, ... the sin of sloth came to include astonishingly few worldly faults and beyond any doubt remained a theological concept'. In Wenzel's judgment, following an exhaustive survey of the relevant literature, the popular understanding of the sin of sloth was still, even by the middle of the fifteenth century, overwhelmingly the neglect of religious duties. As Wenzel sums up: 'in the popular image the sin of sloth remained sloth in God's service, with "God's service" being occasionally extended to include obligations in this world and to society' (Wenzel 1960 & 1967, pp. 95-6).

The state of affairs described by Wenzel can be taken as symptomatic of the Christian morality of pre-Reformation Europe.

Undoubtedly a work ethic existed, but the duty of work, especially work in the secular world, did not rank particularly high compared to other Christian virtues and duties, such as prayer, regular church attendance and confession (for the layman), and above all the way of life of the monk. However, it is easy enough to see how a reformed version of Christianity having a more secular focus might give birth to a work ethic more emphatic and religiously more central than before. Undoubtedly, Protestantism was just such a reformed version of Christianity. This theme will be discussed in the next chapter. On the other hand, given its traditional view of the sinfulness of avarice, it is not at all easy to see how Christianity could give birth to a profit ethic (at one point described by Weber as 'devotion to the calling of making money') (Weber 1930, p. 72). That problem will be the subject of later chapters.

3 Weber's primary Protestant ethic: the work ethic

In this chapter, I shall begin to examine critically Weber's interpretation of the development of religious and economic attitudes after the Reformation. The focus of the chapter will be on the 'primary' Protestant ethic, that is, the work ethic (combined with a general self-denying puritanism). I shall argue (in brief) that Weber was right about the existence of this ethic, but not right about how and why it came into existence. As a result he over-simplified it. I shall also consider how damaging this is to his Thesis.

One question which must be asked immediately is: where is the relevant evidence to be sought? In what countries are the attitudinal elements that figure in the Weber Thesis predicted to manifest themselves? There is little doubt about Weber's own answer: in Britain (or, up till 1707, England and Scotland) and the United States of America. The rationale for this is not hard to understand: Britain was the world's first and then, for a century or more, its leading industrial power, eventually ceding that position to the USA. In both countries, also, ascetic Protestantism was strong, and in both, significantly, industrialism developed so to say spontaneously, rather than as a result of a government-led industrialization policy. To that extent, though only in a rough and ready way, the empirical evidence seems to fit the Weber Thesis (which is, in fact, an attempt to *explain* a correlation that Weber was far from the first to notice). However, two countries have often been claimed as empirical *refutations* of the Thesis – namely Scotland (an independent country at the time of its Reformation in 1560, and up to 1707) and the Dutch Republic, the greatest economic power of the seventeenth century. It is necessary to say something about both these cases.

Scotland can be dealt with quite briefly in this connection. According to Albert Hyma, the history of Calvinism in Scotland is a death-blow to the Weber Thesis. 'Scotland in the seventeenth century became much more thoroughly Calvinistic than England or Holland. But ... the rapid spread of Calvinist ideas and theology did not by any means correspond to the development in commerce and industry ... Trade [in Scotland] lagged far behind ...' (Hyma 1959, p. 104). Hyma is of course right about the thoroughness of the Calvinization of Scotland – indeed, he understates it, since Scotland in the late sixteenth and seventeenth centuries was probably the most Calvinistic nation in the whole of world history. It is also true that in the sixteenth and seventeenth centuries Scotland remained an economic backwater. What, however, may be thought much more significant is the fact that, in the eighteenth and especially the nineteenth centuries this country, hitherto so backward economically, was actually in the forefront of the Industrial Revolution. As the English historian J.A. Froude, writing in 1865, pointed out, in Scotland at the time of the Reformation the middle class was insignificant and almost non-existent. The Scottish middle class was, he says, 'created by religion [i.e. the Reformation] ... and therefore it has been that the print of their origin has gone so deeply into their social constitution' (Froude 1865, p. 12). If Froude is right about the nineteenth century Scottish character, Scotland tends to corroborate Weber rather than refute him.

Hyma also believes that the case of Holland (more properly, the Dutch Republic) refutes Weber (Hyma 1967, pp. 14-23). In this case, it takes a little longer to explain the alleged contradiction between theory and reality, for in the Dutch Republic, the greatest economic power of the seventeenth century, as in Britain and the USA, Calvinism and other ascetic Protestant sects were strong. However, as Hyma and others point out, they were actually strongest in the most economically backward provinces (such as Utrecht and Friesland) and relatively weak in the leading commercial provinces (Holland and Zeeland), and especially in the commercial capital, Amsterdam, above all among its patrician business class, who tended to be attracted to a liberal Arminianism, or else to a relatively secular, non-religious, or at least broadly tolerant attitude (Burke 1974, p. 82; Price 1974, p. 31; Haley 1972, pp. 84-91, 96-9, 107-108). Thus, Weber's critics conclude, the development of capitalism in the seventeenth century Dutch Republic owed little or nothing to Calvinism or ascetic Protestantism.

As a matter of fact, Weber himself agreed with this opinion, but did not see it as damaging to his Thesis; for he did not consider seventeenth century Dutch capitalism to be a case of *modern* Western capitalism (Weber 1930, pp. 200, 217). It was, in fact, entirely a mercantile and financial, rather than an industrial capitalism, and thus more similar to the pre-Reformation capitalism of Venice and other Italian cities, than to the capitalism that gave birth to the Industrial

Revolution. There is thus no more of a problem, for Weber, in explaining how Dutch seventeenth century capitalism could flourish without an ascetic Protestant basis, than in explaining the similar Venetian and Italian pre-Reformation development. If the Dutch Republic does pose a problem for Weber, it is different from that suggested by his critics – not that its capitalism flourished independently of ascetic Protestantism, but why that country *failed* to lead the way to modern industrial capitalism, despite the existence there of great wealth and much Calvinism. However, Weber never argued that ascetic Protestantism was a *sufficient* condition for the rise of modern Western capitalism.

I shall not attempt any further explanation of Dutch history, but will instead focus, as did Weber in *The Protestant Ethic and The Spirit of Capitalism*, on the case of Britain. However, I shall pay a good deal more attention than Weber did to Scotland.[1] One reason for doing so is precisely that, before the Union with England, and for some time after it, the Scottish economy was much poorer and less developed than that of its southern neighbour. This difference in economic development will permit a rough test of the Marxist theory of ideology, which (in contradiction to Weber) holds that ideas tend to reflect the structure of the economy rather than to change it. The Marxist theory would therefore presumably predict that religious ideas in England in the sixteenth and seventeenth centuries would be different from those current in Scotland, would in fact be more friendly to capitalism. As we shall see, a comparison of Scottish Calvinism and English Puritanism lends no support to this hypothesis – if anything, it tends to show that the reverse is the case. That, however, will not become fully apparent until detailed consideration is given, in later chapters, to the crucial question of the profit ethic.

As I have argued, it is essential, in evaluating the Weber Thesis, to distinguish what I have called the 'primary' from the 'secondary' Protestant ethic, or the work ethic from the profit ethic. There is another, perhaps more perspicuous way to express this distinction, and to show the contrast between the two: in the primary Protestant ethic, one's work in the world is viewed as a calling in the religious sense: in the secondary Protestant ethic, the making of money (as much money as one honestly can) is viewed as such a calling. The former, I suggested, is *a priori* a good deal easier to understand than the latter. For the moment, however, I wish to draw a different lesson, relating to the primary Protestant ethic only. In the previous chapter, I argued that pre-Reformation Christianity already contained, so to speak, a work ethic waiting to be (fully) born. However, Weber's Thesis about the primary Protestant ethic is not simply that the Reformation (or ascetic Protestantism) gave birth to it, but that it gave birth to it in a particularly powerful form, by (to mix metaphors) marrying it with the idea of the calling. Both these aspects – ethical secularization, and the calling – need to be borne in mind. Both are due, in the first instance, to Luther.

Weber recognized this, without however particularly distinguishing the two elements (see above, page 5, second paragraph), but the point can bear some elaboration. So far as ethical secularization is concerned, Weber dwelt particularly on Luther's attack on monasticism, and his contrasting elevation of worldly duties (Weber 1930, p 81). Equally striking, however, in Luther's secularization of ethics is his attack on the priestly class of the old Church, headed of course by the Pope. The Protestant doctrine of the priesthood of all believers is well enough known, but this egalitarian theological concept is only one aspect of Luther's crusade against priestly pretensions. Another is his redefinition of virtue, which is expressed in a form that is nothing short of vitriolic in his Greater Catechism. After a lengthy discussion of the Ten Commandments, which he calls 'a summary of Divine instruction', Luther's Catechism continues as follows:

> And now let us see what our great saints have to boast about concerning their holy orders, and the great and hard tasks which they have invented and set themselves, while neglecting the Commandments ... Works [prescribed by the Commandments] are of no account or importance in the eyes of the world, for they do not appear extraordinary or pompous: and are not bound to any special times, places, rites and ceremonies, but are the common work of everyday life in our intercourse with our neighbour and accordingly make no great show. Other works may make one gaze with eyes and ears, and this is furthered by the show they make [in which] folk dress themselves out that all they do may dazzle and amaze. They burn incense, chant, jingle bells, light candles and tapers, so that one cannot see or hear anything. For a priest standing in a golden surplice or a layman lying all day on his knees in church, this they call an admirable work that none can praise enough. But when a poor little maid attends to a young child and honestly does what is asked of her, that is considered nothing ... Is this not detestable arrogance? (Luther 1896, pp. 90-1)

In this passage, Luther's contempt for priestly splendour and rituals, contrasted with his respect for the honest work of the maid, clearly manifests a new, more secular conception of Christian ethics, but without any invocation of the calling. Let us remind ourselves just why this concept is so important. The reason is that it brings together, and even conflates, two ideas, worldly behaviour, and the salvation of the soul. As Weber explains, in two lengthy and important footnotes to Chapter Three of his famous essay, the words 'calling' and 'vocation' (in Latin *vocatio*) had, for centuries before the Reformation, been connected with the idea of salvation – they referred to 'the call of the Gospel to eternal salvation' (Weber 1930, pp. 204-210). Luther continued to use 'calling' (*Beruf*) in this sense, as well as in the new sense of a Christian's worldly task.[2] The same dual use was continued by Luther's Calvinist successors – in the lexicon of orthodox Calvinism, the process in which God, 'by his word and spirit', gives saving faith to the elect, is known as 'Effectual Calling' (as stated for example in the Westminster Confession of Faith of 1647) (Weber 1930, pp. 99-100). But the terminological situation is actually slightly more complex. According to the Westminster Confession, the effectual calling of the elect 'determines them to that which is good'. In accordance with the doctrine that true faith manifests itself in godly conduct, a Christian is thus called by God to a certain way of life, and that way of life is the Christian calling. Furthermore, the Christian calling includes two elements: the general calling (duties common to all Christians) and the particular calling (those inhering in one's particular station in life). The connection between calling and salvation, so central to Weber's Thesis, is made manifest in a brief Biblical passage that was continually quoted by the preachers of the Reformed Christian churches: 'Use all diligence to make thy calling and election sure'.[3]

This entire vocabulary and conceptual apparatus were already in place in both England and Scotland before 1600. Perhaps the first fully elaborated statement of Weber's 'primary Protestant ethic' was provided by one of the leaders of English Puritanism, William Perkins, in his *Treatise of the Vocations or Callings of Men*. In a rigorous and systematic treatment of his subject, Perkins distinguished between the two kinds of vocation or calling – general and particular – the latter being defined as 'a certain kind of life imposed on men by God for the common good' (Perkins 1970, pp. 446-7, 451). Everyone, therefore, must have his or her particular calling: 'Whatsoever is not done within the compass of a calling is not of faith'. Perkins' use of the concept of the calling is an almost perfect expression of Weber's primary Protestant ethic. It expresses an explicit work ethic, for 'every man must do the duties of his calling *with diligence*' (emphasis added). There are, Perkins continues, 'two damnable sins that are contrary to this diligence. The first is idleness whereby the duties of our callings and the occasions of glorifying God are neglected or omitted. The second is slothfulness, whereby they are performed slackly or carelessly ...' (Perkins 1970, p. 450). Perkins' account of men's particular callings also expresses what I have called the ethic of puritanism, for he insists that not every way of making a living is a calling: excluded ways are, for example, 'by usury, by carding and dicing, by maintaining houses of gaming, by plays and such-like ...' as well as 'by making foreign and fond fashions of attire, which serve for no use but to be displayed flags and banners either of folly, or pride, or wantonness'. 'Such miserable courses of living' are contrary to the will of God (Perkins 1970, pp. 447, 462). Most telling of all is the way in which Perkins makes absolutely explicit the link between this conception of good works and proof of salvation, precisely through the concept of the calling: 'If thou wouldest have signs and tokens of thy election and salvation, thou must fetch them from the constant practice of thy two callings (general and particular) jointly together' (Perkins 1970, p. 457).

Perkins' joining together of the 'two callings' has a further implication relevant to the Weber Thesis: one's performance of one's particular calling must be governed by the general obligations of Christian life in the world, such as norms of honesty. 'The main end of our lives' says Perkins 'is to serve God in the serving of man in the work of our callings' (Perkins 1970, p. 457). Therefore, 'he abuseth his calling whosoever he be that, against the end thereof, employs it for himself, seeking only his own and not the common good'. Honesty is thus prescribed not (as in Weber's 'spirit of capitalism') as 'the best policy' or a means to maximize profit, but rather as a restriction on profit-seeking. We must, Perkins says, avoid all 'injustice' – the merchant and tradesman, for example, must never cheat by using false weights and measures, by lying, by 'setting a [false] gloss on wares by powdering'; he must eschew 'all manner of bad dealing' (Perkins 1970, pp. 449, 464, 467-8). Such dishonest practices are, Perkins says, born of the sin of covetousness – a very traditional argument, now applied to the definition of the particular calling, and constantly reiterated by later Puritan writers on the subject.

It is of interest to find doctrines very similar to those of Perkins, if less systematically expressed, in the writings of his Scottish contemporary, Robert Rollock, who was Professor of Theology at the University of Edinburgh from 1587.[4] For example: 'It is not the Lord's will that any man should be idle in this world. It is his will that all men all their days be painfully occupied in some calling, wherein they may both glorify God and do good unto men'. 'When, with a simple and upright heart, we are labouring in our callings we are serving the Lord' (Rollock 1849, Vol. II, pp. 693-4, 588). To Rollock, it is just this behaviour that is the proof of true faith and the guarantee of personal salvation. 'Mark how ye shall know whether a man love Christ or not – a king, a minister, any professor whatever. Would ye have a token? Look if he be faithful in his calling ... By their works shall ye know them ... when thou seest a man well occupied in his own calling ... certainly thou mayest say "Yon man loves Christ"' (Rollock 1849, Vol. II, p. 616). 'If thou discharge thy commission faithfully in thy calling ... so shalt thou be welcome when thou shalt meet with the Lord, and he shall accept well of thee. [If we are] well occupied, and walk carefully in that calling that he hath placed us in ... then, when the Lord of glory shall appear, whom we have served in this life, our souls and bodies shall enjoy the full fruition of his presence in heaven ...' (Rollock 1849, Vol. II, p. 415). These passages demonstrate the centrality in Rollock's thought of the calling, the work ethic, and the link of both with eternal salvation. Nor would it be difficult to cite elements of the 'puritan' ethic from Rollock's teachings.

We may conclude that, by the end of the sixteenth century, Weber's primary Protestant ethic was fully established both in England and Scotland. But did it come into existence in the way Weber asserted? Not quite, I think. A striking feature of Weber's argument is that, because of his 'ideal type' methodology, he tends always to represent the teachings of religious groups as internally more or less consistent at any given time.[5] True, these teachings may change, as, Weber argued, Calvinist doctrine changed from Calvin himself to Beza, but each successive version is presented as internally coherent. Weber's methodology is understandable, since it enables him to present his argument with maximum force and clarity, but it can be misleading. It fails to do justice to the fact that confusion and contradiction are the normal condition of theoretical mankind. So it is, I suggest, in the present case. According to Weber, Calvin was personally unworried by the problem of assurance of salvation, despite his view that the elect 'differ externally in this life in no way from the damned; and even all the subjective experiences of the chosen are ... possible for the damned with the single exception of that *finaliter* expectant, trusting faith. The elect thus are and remain God's invisible Church' (Weber 1930, p. 110). Only with Beza's succession and the spread of Calvinism among 'the broad mass of ordinary men' did the need for an objective proof of salvation motivate the introduction of godly living as the sign of true faith. Actually this is not so. The truth is that both of these contradictory doctrines were taught, not only by Calvin but by all the Reformers, including Luther. This can be illustrated quite easily. I believe it can also be explained.

Let me first of all document Calvin's own inconsistency on the question. Here is a passage that conforms to Weber's account. 'The elect are not gathered into the fold of Christ by calling immediately after birth ... Before they are gathered to that chief Shepherd, they go astray ... differing in no respect from others, except in being protected by the special mercy of God ... If you observe them, therefore, you will see the posterity of Adam, partaking of the corruption of the whole species'. Yet Calvin also asserts that 'Christ regenerates to a blessed life those whom he justifies, and after rescuing them from the dominion of sin, hands them over to the domain of righteousness ... and trains them by His spirit into obedience to His will ...' The elect are 'elected to be holy'. Hence 'the saints' can have confidence in their good works 'as marks of their calling whence they infer their election,' while correspondingly 'The reprobate ... by their continual crimes ... confirm by clear signs that God's judgment has already been pronounced upon them'. But are the signs so clear? It seems not, after all, for according to Calvin Judas is among the elect, simply by virtue of God's predestination: and 'it daily happens that they who appear to belong to Christ, fall away from him again, and sink into ruin'. And in general, Calvin admits, the reprobate may have 'similar signs of calling with the elect'; what they necessarily lack, he continues, is not the external signs but 'certain assurance of grace', derivable from the word of the Gospel and an 'accompanying illumination of the Spirit' (Calvin 1813, Vol. II pp. 259, 455; Calvin 1968, pp. 163, 192, 196, 213).

Calvin, then, explicitly but not consistently, already linked good works with proof of salvation. But did his conception of good works involve the particular earthly calling and the work ethic? Some critics of Weber have doubted this, but their doubts are unfounded. Calvin tells us that 'The Lord ... hath appointed to all their particular duties in different spheres of life [and] hath styled such spheres of life *vocations* or *callings* ... So necessary is this distinction that in His sight all our actions are estimated by it' (Calvin 1813, Vol. II, p. 195). Also, 'It is a praiseworthy virtue diligently to discharge the duties of our office. It is not the will of the Lord that we should be like blocks of wood, or that we should keep our arms folded, without doing anything' (Calvin 1843, p. 104). The calling is explicitly linked with a work ethic in a comment on the parable of the labourers in the vineyard, from which Calvin infers that 'Man was created for activity ... Each has his divinely appointed station ... Our whole life is useless, and we are justly condemned of laziness, until we frame our life to the command and calling of God' (Calvin 1972, Vol. II, pp. 265-6). 'Indolence and idle conduct are cursed by God' (Calvin 1961, p. 418). While Calvin did not, so far as I know, explicitly suggest that diligence in one's particular calling proves election, that inference could easily be drawn from those elements of Weber's primary Protestant ethic that are, as has been shown, explicit in his writings. On the other hand, it is just as explicitly contradicted by others.

Calvin's inconsistencies on the signs of election – or the relation between faith and works – are echoed by his English followers. A good example is William Perkins. Perkins, whose *Treatise of the Callings or Vocations of Men* was quoted above, is also the author of a *Treatise Tending unto a Declaration Whether a Man be in the Estate of Damnation or in the Estate of Grace*. In the latter, Perkins expresses his views through a 'true Christian', Eusebius, who at one point claims to have 'some assurance, in spite of the devil, that I do pertain to the kingdom of heaven' – despite the fact, that is, 'that when temptations come I cannot stand, when I have sinned faith is feeble ... when my neighbour needeth my help ... then my love is cold' (Perkins 1970, pp. 366, 372). On what can Eusebius' assurance be based? Possibly on the principle that 'it is a good token of the grace of God in you' if 'you are grieved with a godly sorrow for your sins' (Perkins 1970, p. 366). Yet on the other hand: 'Here is a good way to know whether we have faith or not ... Faith is never severed from hope and charity ... The office of love [i.e. charity] is to pour out the same goodness that it hath received from God upon her neighbour ...' (Perkins 1970, p. 373). For Eusebius, the true Christian (as his friend Timotheus points out), 'faith and hope towards God and charity towards our neighbour are inseparable'. As with Calvin, there is an oscillation between conflicting positions. Similar equivocations could be endlessly cited from the works of other divines.[6]

Why exactly is this so? One reason, no doubt, is the problem Weber mentioned, of reconciling Protestant solifideism (salvation by faith alone) with the need of ordinary Christians for a clear, objective criterion of salvation.[7] But there is also, I suggest, another reason. One of the most strongly held tenets of the Protestant Reformers is the utter sinfulness of man. The doctrine of salvation by faith alone is a corollary of this. Works are useless for salvation because men, since Adam's sin, are utterly corrupt, incapable (by their own nature) of obeying God's law, therefore incapable of meriting salvation by good works (or anything else). According to Luther, followed by Calvin, every human being merits eternal damnation. But not all are damned, for God in his mercy has chosen to save some (the Calvinist 'elect'). The saved receive their salvation by God's free grace; they receive from God, through the Holy Spirit, a saving faith in Jesus Christ.

Doctrinal questions apart, what are the psychological attractions of such a view of the human condition? It is not hard to find a plausible answer. If one believes unquestioningly in God's eternal rewards and punishments, and has at the same time a deep sense of personal sinfulness (as appears to have been Luther's case), the Protestant position serves to ease the fear of damnation: it teaches that one may be a sinner and yet be saved (for all the saved are sinners). Logically, it is perfectly consistent so far. But it also, at the same time, gives rise to serious practical problems, whose resolution requires that logical consistency be sacrificed. One problem arises from an implication noted by Weber, namely, that the saved and the damned are outwardly indistinguishable – all, equally, are sinners. From this, there is an obvious antinomian conclusion, which many did not hesitate to draw – that one might as well sin.[8] Neither Luther nor Calvin, being socially responsible men, could entertain this inference for a moment. Nor was it enough just to inveigh against antinomianism; they had to provide a psychological sanction against it: they had to *deny* that there is no difference in the worldly behaviour of the saved and the damned. It is faith that saves; but true faith manifests itself in good works. Sinners, it would therefore appear, cannot be saved. This revised position is an improvement from the point of view of social control. On the other hand, it sacrifices all the psychological consolations offered by the original one to the troubled believer. The reformers, therefore, especially in their capacity as pastoral counsellors, found it impossible to hold to the position that sinfulness is proof of damnation. In fact, they found it impossible to adhere consistently to either position. The problem, and the danger of contradiction to which it leads, lie deep in the very fundamentals of Protestantism.

This being so, we might expect to find inconsistencies in the works of Luther, similar to those noted above in Calvin and Perkins. And indeed, this is precisely what we do find. Thus, on the one hand Luther wrote: 'A Christian is not someone who has no sin ... ; he is someone to whom, because of his faith in Christ, God does not impute his sin'; and on the other: 'We, being justified by faith, do good works, through which our call and election are confirmed and made more certain day by day ...' Another passage of Luther refers both to 'internal testimony' which gives the heart 'complete certainty that it is in a state of grace', and also to 'external signs' by which 'we are assured and confirmed ... that we are in a state of grace'. Confusingly, although the external signs referred to are mostly overt actions (e.g. 'to help a needy brother'), they also include subjective attitudes ('not to take delight in sin'). Finally, to complete the confusion, Luther adds: 'The wicked have these signs too, but not in a pure way' (Luther 1968, p. 105; Luther 1963, pp. 260, 378-9).

Were the Reformers able to clear up this confusion? Up to a point, but only up to a point. One popular resolution of the dilemma is as follows.[9] As we have seen, man and all his works are inherently sinful, and hence the human capacity for good works (as for faith) comes not from man's nature but from the Holy Spirit. However, the infusion of the Holy Spirit does not annihilate a person's corrupt and sinful nature (often referred to as the 'old man'). The regenerate are, rather, those who feel the effects of the Spirit, whose lives, therefore, are a continual warfare between the purifying Spirit and the sinful flesh. They are still tempted to sin, and they still sin. The work of the Spirit in them manifests itself as a hatred of their sins, and in the struggle to overcome their natural sinfulness – the process known as 'sanctification' – but the victory would never be total in this life. This doctrine may be looked on as an attempt to avoid the evils of antinomianism on the one side, and despair on the other. Sinners can be saved, but only if they sincerely resist sin. But it is hard to say, now, whether there is any objective criterion of salvation, or whether it is purely subjective. In fact, it seems that the Protestant reformers never squared this circle, but continually oscillated between subjective and objective criteria of grace.

The point can be suitably illustrated by the Confession of Faith drawn up by the Scottish Reformers, and ratified by the Estates of the Realm in Edinburgh in 1560. It is worth quoting at some length from this Confession. Chapter XIII contains the following:

> The cause of Good Works we confess to be, not our free will, but the Spirit of the Lord Jesus who, dwelling in our hearts by true faith, brings forth such good works as God hath prepared for us to walk into; for this we most boldly affirm, that blasphemy it is to say that Christ Jesus abides in the hearts of such as in whom there is no spirit of Sanctification. And therefore we fear not to affirm that murderers, oppressors, cruel persecutors, adulterers, whoremongers, filthy persons, idolaters, drunkards, thieves and all workers of iniquity, have neither true faith, neither any portion of the spirit of Sanctification, which proceedeth from the Lord Jesus, so long as they obstinately continue in their wickedness. For how soon that ever the Spirit of the Lord Jesus (which God's elect children receive by true faith) takes possession in the heart of any man, so soon does he regenerate and renew the same man; so that he begins to hate that which before he loved, and begins to love that which before he hated; and from that comes that continual battle which is betwixt the flesh and the spirit in God's children:

while the flesh and natural man (according to its own corruption) lusts for things pleasing and delectable unto the self ... and at every moment is prone and ready to offend the Majesty of God. But the Spirit of God, which giveth witnessing to our spirit, that we are the sons of God, makes us to resist the devil, to abhor filthy pleasures, to groan in God's presence for deliverance from this bondage of corruption: and finally so to triumph over sin that it reign not in our mortal bodies. This battle has (sic) not the carnal men, being destitute of God's spirit; but do follow and obey sin with greediness, and without repentance ... But the sons of God ... do fight against sin, do sob and moan, when they perceive themselves tempted to iniquity; and if they fall, they rise again with earnest and unfeigned repentance.

The authors of this passage show a strong hostility to 'workers of iniquity' and an apparent desire to deny them any hope of salvation, so long as they do not mend their ways ('obstinately continue in their wickedness'). But the sons of God, too, are tempted to iniquity, and may commit it. The difference is that their iniquities lead to 'earnest and unfeigned repentance' – a purely subjective criterion. Another passage, however, appears to state an objective criterion of regeneration: it makes us after many battles 'finally so to triumph over sin that it reign not in our mortal bodies'. But this suggestion that the regenerate man finally conquers his sinful tendencies is directly contradicted by another section of the Confession (in Chapter XV):

Our nature is so corrupt, so weak and imperfect, that we are never able to fulfil the works of the law in perfection: yea, 'If we say we have no sin (even after we are regenerate) we deceive ourselves, and the verity of God is not into us ...[10]

The apparently inescapable equivocations on the connections between divine grace and godly behaviour on earth that are found in the Scottish Confession of Faith are similar to those noted earlier in Luther, Calvin and Perkins. Unlike Calvin and Perkins, however, the Confession, naturally enough, does not concern itself with the particular calling or the work ethic. What about Luther? Weber, of course, stressed the importance of his conception of the calling, but Luther in fact went further than this, explicitly linking the earthly calling with assurance of salvation; for among his 'external signs' of grace (see above, p. 36) is that one 'do one's duty according to one's calling in a manly way, in faith and joy' (he adds that it is one's own calling one must serve, not another's) (Luther 1963, pp. 378-9). Furthermore, Luther's conception of this calling is linked to a work ethic: 'To be sure, God does everything: but we too must do what belongs to our calling ... It is God's command that you should do your duty, and He wants to work through you. Therefore, you must devote yourself to your work and duty with all your strength and attention'. 'In this life ... a man cannot enjoy leisure' (Luther 1961, p. 290; Luther 1968, pp. 16-17).

These views of Luther amount to a more or less complete endorsement of Weber's primary Protestant ethic. Indeed, if we compare Luther and Calvin, it is Luther who seems to match it more completely, in that Luther (but apparently not Calvin) explicitly linked diligent performance of the duties of one's earthly calling with assurance of salvation. (Admittedly, other statements of Luther's, as we have seen, contradict the primary Protestant ethic, but exactly the same is true of Calvin and even of its systematizer, Perkins.) This gives rise to a problem. Weber, as we know, portrayed Calvin and Calvinism as the fountainhead of Protestant inner-worldly asceticism, but excluded Luther and Lutheranism entirely from that category (Weber 1930, pp. 85-6). Luther plays an important part in his argument, but only in his explanation of the emergence of the Protestant ethic, not as an example of it. How can this be justified? Weber himself argued that 'Luther's concept of the calling remained traditionalistic', that is, he saw it more as a fate to be accepted than a 'task set by God' – in contrast, presumably, to the later spokesmen of the Protestant ethic. Arguably, some excessively fine distinctions are involved here, as well as some very difficult quantitative judgments, both as to the balance between different elements in Luther's teaching, and as to differences between the balance in Luther and in others. Critics of Weber, such as H.M. Robertson, have been unable to discern the change postulated by Weber in the connotations of the calling (Robertson 1933, pp. 6-14).

Be that as it may, there is another and much more obvious difference between Luther and Lutheranism on the one hand, and Calvin and the Reformed Churches on the other, namely their respective attitudes to the institution of confession (mentioned by Weber only in passing) (Weber 1930, pp. 106, 240). The Lutherans, naturally, greatly altered the medieval practice, which was based on a conception of priesthood which they repudiated, but they did not abolish the confession. Luther, indeed, greatly expanded it, in a startlingly radical application of the doctrine of the priesthood of all believers (an application which, however, appears to contradict another, even more basic, Protestant doctrine, salvation by faith alone).[11] According to Luther, confession is a useful and necessary institution, but not a priestly monopoly: absolution can be received from any fellow-Christian, indeed it must be granted if requested, without the imposition of any penances (Lea 1896, p. 516). Article 11 of the Augsburg Confession of Faith of 1530 explicitly defends private confession and absolution, while Article 25 even states that admission to communion among Lutherans is dependent on confession and absolution (by a minister, as was made explicit in Lutheran church regulations). By contrast, although Calvin's own views on confession were surprisingly equivocal, any confession other than to God Himself was firmly and explicitly repudiated by his Reformed Church followers as early as 1566, only two years after his death (Lea 1896, pp. 519-520). Not surprisingly, Luther's remarkably democratic version of the institution of confession did not long prevail, so that, by the early seventeenth century power of absolution in the Lutheran Churches was effectively confined to pastors. Gradually, too, all private absolution fell into abeyance, and in modern times the institution survives only in the form of a ritualistic general absolution of congregations from the pulpit (Lea 1896, p. 517). This history is, I suggest, of some relevance to the Weber Thesis: it gives reasons why, in terms of Weber's argument, Lutheranism, in its original incarnation, fell short of exemplifying the full Protestant ethic, while also suggesting that in later centuries it may have moved, so to speak, within its terms, as private confession fell into desuetude.[12]

One major question remains to be considered before this discussion of Weber's primary Protestant ethic can be considered complete – the most important question of all. The main theme of this chapter has been that, while the primary Protestant ethic was indeed clearly enunciated in England and Scotland by the end of the sixteenth century, most notably by William Perkins, other and conflicting ideas were also expressed by the Calvinists of these countries, including Perkins himself. Does this weaken, or even refute the Weber Thesis? It depends exactly what this question means. Undoubtedly, the Thesis over-simplifies the situation. On the other hand, it is arguable that a more complex account, truer to the complex reality, actually strengthens the Thesis, if the Thesis is that the teachings of ascetic Protestantism motivated diligence in the earthly calling. If one grants to Weber the motivating power of concern for the fate of one's eternal soul, then the more complex account of ascetic Protestant teaching is roughly as follows. Believers were taught that godly behaviour indicated salvation, sinful behaviour damnation (this is congruent with the Weber Thesis). But this teaching might have lead to despair, so they were also told that it is not the whole truth – sinners can be among the saved. That is, they can be among the saved if they hate their sin and sincerely fight against it (all of this remains a *sign* of salvation, not a *means* to it, according to Protestant dogma). This further teaching, I have argued, confuses the issue, in the sense that it makes it far more difficult to be confident about one's state of grace. The more complex picture, in other words, is damaging to that assurance the need for which was so strongly emphasized by Weber and the criteria for which, according to Weber, were provided because, psychologically, they had to be provided. But, I suggest, it does *not* reduce the motivation to godly behaviour, but rather the reverse, and precisely because assurance, while still sought, is so much harder to achieve. And if godly behaviour includes – must include – diligence in one's earthly calling, a point on which the Protestant preachers were well-nigh unanimous, then that behaviour would likewise be all the more strongly motivated.

4 Weber's secondary Protestant ethic: the profit ethic

Before moving on to discuss what I have called Weber's secondary Protestant ethic – the Protestant profit ethic – it will be useful to draw some morals from the previous chapter. That chapter, I suggest, reveals two related weaknesses in Weber's argument, one of which has quite often been noted, the other I think less so. The former is that Weber's ideal type methodology tends to over-simplify a complex reality, and (in the present case) to exaggerate the logical consistency of ascetic Protestant teachings. Relatedly, Weber contends or assumes that this logical consistency was *necessary* in order that these teachings should perform the psychological function ascribed to them in his Thesis.[1] In other words, it was a psychological necessity for Calvin's followers and members of other ascetic Protestant sects to be given a clear and unambiguous indicator of their state of grace – clear distinguishing marks between the saved and the damned. In this way, the argument continues, Protestant laymen were motivated to manifest the signs of grace in their own lives, through behaviour pleasing to God, including especially diligence in their earthly callings. My conclusion in the previous chapter is different. No clear, consistent sign of grace, of salvation or damnation, was offered by the spokesmen of ascetic Protestantism – for good or at least understandable reasons, their teachings on the subject were not consistent. Nevertheless, this does not mean that their followers were not motivated by anxiety about salvation to behave in a godly way, as defined by the preachers – on the contrary, it is probable that the inconsistency and uncertainty on the subject was a motivator as powerful or more powerful than consistency and certainty would have been.

This point is not trivial: in fact, I shall contend that it has in large part skewed the debate about the Weber Thesis, and even Weber's own statement of it. I am referring, now, to the secondary Protestant ethic, or rather one part of it. For, if what is seen as crucial is the provision of a clear and unambiguous criterion of salvation, Weber's argument could hardly stop at or rest on the primary Protestant ethic alone. Hard, diligent work in the earthly calling is simply not a sufficiently clear-cut, objective criterion. *How* hard must one work? How diligent must one be? The anxious, earnest Protestant pictured by Weber must have continued to be tormented by uncertainty. Of course, this would be likely to make him work all the harder – but not necessarily enable him to achieve assurance. According to Weber, some clear criterion is still needed: and what more natural than *success* in one's calling, in the clear objective terms of money profit? And, Weber argued, precisely this further step was taken: 'The certainty ... that God would bless His own in this life – ... and also in the material sense – ... came to be of great importance for Puritanism' (Weber 1930, p. 164). I shall argue that this claim of Weber's is inaccurate, or rather is a misleading half-truth. Furthermore, it diverts attention from the real issue, which is not clear signs of election, but effective motivation to specific patterns of behaviour. Here again, clarity and consistency on signs of election are not to be found: but neither are they necessary.

It is fairly easy to see why clarity and consistency on this issue are not to be expected from the spokesmen of ascetic Protestantism. Partly, the reasons have to do with psychological and social factors of a more or less universal kind unrelated to Protestant doctrine; but there are doctrinal reasons also. Let us begin with reasons why one might expect to find preachers asserting a correlation between divine grace and worldly success. At the most general level is a powerful tendency stressed, ironically, by Weber himself in another context: the tendency for moral cosmologies of all sorts to include the idea that forces or powers active in the universe bring it about that virtue is rewarded and vice or sin punished. As Weber pointed out, the most brilliant example of this sort of theodicy (brilliant not least in its immunity to refutation) is provided by Hinduism, through its concept of reincarnation: one's state and fate in this life are a reward or punishment for merit, or otherwise, manifested in a previous existence (Weber 1965-6, p. 113). The notion that worldly prosperity and divine grace, hence worldly prosperity and godly conduct, are correlated, can be seen as a similar idea translated into Protestant concepts and vocabulary (which, of course, lack any notion of reincarnation). All such theodicies, obviously, are justifications of economic and social inequality, and can be looked on in two ways. They can be seen as rendering human life and fortune in the world *meaningful* rather than arbitrary (virtue is rewarded, vice punished); or they can be seen as transparently ideological in the Marxist sense of serving the interests of wealthy classes (wealth is a merited reward, poverty a merited punishment). If, as Weber tells us, 'God blesseth his trade' became a stock remark about the successful self-made Puritan businessman, it is not only Marxists who might be inclined to reply by adapting some famous words of Mandy Rice-Davies: 'Well, they would say that, wouldn't they?'[2]

There is another, simpler and more obvious, reason why Puritan preachers might be expected to assert a correlation between salvation, or godliness, and worldly success, which in essence has nothing to do with Puritanism – namely, that they wished to encourage godly behaviour as they defined it, and to discourage what they saw as sin, and could scarcely be expected to resist the temptation to use temporal promises and threats in order to achieve their desired ends. This purely pragmatic reason can be combined with a doctrinal one: that *certain* forms of godly and sinful behaviour, as conceived by ascetic Protestantism – indeed, precisely those that make up Weber's primary Protestant ethic, such as the virtue of diligent work in one's calling, and the sins of idleness, self-indulgence and extravagance – are genuinely likely to favour economic success and failure respectively. This point is obvious, and has often been noted by Weber's commentators, but its precise significance has less often, I believe, been understood. I shall be returning to it later. But in the meantime, let us note two highly serviceable Biblical passages that were continually quoted by Calvinist and Puritan divines: that in Timothy which says that godliness 'hath the promises of this life' as well as of 'the life to come'; and the one in Proverbs, that 'The hand of the diligent maketh rich'.[3] Both of these passages suggest that religious virtue brings worldly success, but in significantly different ways: the former specifies neither the virtue nor any mechanism for its reward other than divine Providence; the latter picks out a form of virtue which, as we saw, is likely by purely natural processes to bring worldly prosperity.

More accurately, it makes worldly prosperity more likely – it certainly does not guarantee it. This too is obvious, just as it was equally obvious, to anyone with the most casual acquaintance with real life, that virtue or godliness in general is *not* highly correlated with worldly prospering. (The Puritan theodicy, unlike the Hindu, is open to empirical refutation.) These facts were also obvious to the Puritan preachers and divines, who knew too that they were obvious to their lay followers. Some explanation, therefore, had to be provided, especially to those obedient Christians (there must have been many) who experienced worldly failure and misfortune, which would make sense of their situation. In order to cope with this problem, Puritan spokesmen found it necessary (indeed natural) to belittle the importance of the rewards of this world by comparison with those of the next, and to *deny* any necessary correlation between worldly success and eternal salvation. In part, as we shall shortly see, their argument took the form of appropriate glossing and interpretation of God's promises to His elect.

Before turning to the detailed evidence, however, it should be pointed out that, in addition to the pragmatic ones, there were also good doctrinal reasons why ascetic Protestantism could not be expected to see reliable evidence of godliness in worldly prosperity, even if that prosperity resulted from the practice of one's earthly calling. In the first place, as the preachers knew, such gains could well be the result of sinful rather than godly behaviour – of that deceit and dishonesty in trade against which they never ceased to fulminate. Obviously, prosperity achieved by such means could not be a sign of salvation. Secondly, as Weber himself emphasized, without apparently seeing the full significance of the point, wealth, however virtuously obtained, was always regarded by Calvinists and Puritans, with almost total unanimity, as a danger to its possessor, because a temptation to all manner of sinful behaviour – self-indulgence, luxury, idleness, debauchery (Weber 1930, p. 157). Undeniably, wealth is potentially a means to such courses, so the fears of the preachers are entirely comprehensible. But if, as for example, William Perkins proclaimed, riches 'are in some men occasions of sin' (Perkins 1609, Vol. II, p. 145); if, as the Scot John Abernethy wrote, 'The heart too much enjoying prosperity is deprived of grace, and is loosed to all impiety' (Abernethy 1622, pp. 141-2); then riches and prosperity cannot be a reliable index of virtue, or of salvation.[4]

A third doctrinal reason against the correlation of wealth and salvation has been mentioned by a number of Weber's critics,[5] namely, some elements inherent in the doctrine of the particular calling itself. To be sure, this doctrine was endlessly used by the Puritans and Calvinists to enjoin diligence in one's worldly task, but this was not its only function. It was also a way of counselling contentment with one's worldly status. In this world we all have our various God-given tasks to perform, some high, some low; some men are (in worldly terms) great and mighty, others humble; but all lawful callings, however great or humble, being appointed by God, are of equal value in His eyes. Hence one should not be distressed by the humbleness of one's earthly task, or by one's lowly situation in the world; diligent performance of the duties of one's calling, however meagre the material rewards, is pleasing to God and, perhaps, a sign of grace. As William Perkins wrote: 'Let [men of mean place and calling] consider, that in serving of men, by poor and base duties, they serve God: and that therefore their service is not base in his sight: and though their reward from men may be little, yet the reward at God's hand shall not be wanting' (Perkins 1608-9, Vol. I, p. 734). According to the Scot William Colvill, Christ himself 'came in a low condition, for the comfort of many of the godly, who are born and live in a poor and low condition here on earth: their low and despicable condition in the world, shall not be any prejudice to the salvation of their souls' (Colvill 1673, p. 7). And Richard Baxter himself counselled: 'If thou be called to the poorest laborious calling, do not carnally murmur at it ... nor imagine that God accepteth the less of thy work and thee' (Baxter 1673, p. 450).

Remarks such as these are exceedingly common, and seem like a clear refutation of Weber. However, the issue is not so clear-cut. As I have argued, ascetic Protestant spokesmen had pragmatic and doctrinal reasons both to assert a correlation between wealth and godliness or salvation, and to deny it. One would therefore expect their teachings taken as a whole to be contradictory. This is indeed the case. In fact, the inconsistency on this point is dramatic, not only between different Protestant spokesmen, but within the writings of individual spokesmen, and even within individual works written by them. It is actually quite hard to find a Puritan writer or preacher who did not make contradictory statements on this point. Compare, for example, the quotation from Perkins above with the following, also from Perkins: 'The obedience of the Gospel is it that makes every man in his trade, office and calling to prosper ... On the contrary they are wretched and miserable that live without the Gospel,' a claim that Perkins supports by numerous references to Biblical chapter and verse (Perkins 1617, p. 290). Lewis Bayley, another important English Puritan spokesman, and author of the very widely read *Practice of Piety*, apparently agreed: 'To all things in Heaven and Earth [the godly man] has a sure title in this life [and] the life to come' (Bayley, n.d., pp. 67-70). But John Calvin himself seems to have thought otherwise: 'All whom the Lord hath chosen and honoured with admission to the society of his saints, ought to prepare themselves for a life hard, laborious, unquiet and replete with numerous and various calamities ...' (Calvin 1813, p. 172). The Scot George Hutcheson both agreed and disagreed for, on the one hand, 'Piety hath the promises even of this life', but on the other, 'Men's prosperity is no evidence of divine approbation ... for if it were so, it would not be dispensed as it is' (Hutcheson 1669, pp. 5, 304). John Preston appears equally inconsistent, or more so: in one work he wrote that 'God makes us rich by being diligent in our callings', in another that 'This claim [that a diligent hand maketh rich] doth not always hold; God breaks it many times' (Preston 1641, pp. 254 f; Preston 1636, p. 22).

But how could this be? How could God break his promises to His elect, or violate His own words as revealed in Holy Writ? Clearly such a thing was impossible, and it was incumbent on the preachers to reconcile the Biblical promises, which they themselves so often emphasized, with the empirical facts of life. Nor did they shirk this responsibility. How did they set about discharging it? I shall note four lines of argument that were frequently adopted.

First, it was suggested that, although one might, at any given moment, observe wicked men flourishing 'as the green bay tree' while the godly were wretched and miserable, the latter should take comfort from the consideration that such an anomalous situation was merely temporary: in His own good time God in His wrath would snatch away the unmerited wealth of the wicked, and reward, materially, the virtue of His children. Robert Rollock pointed out that 'God often times delays the success of the labours of his own ... to the end that in his own appointed time he may give it more abundantly to their greater comfort' (Rollock 1849, Vol. II, p. 584). George Hutcheson used a similar argument to remove the appearance of contradiction in his remarks cited above: 'Some of the wicked [suffer] loss of their wealth and estate [which] shall come to the innocent and righteous' (Hutcheson 1669, p. 395). Of course, we already know that wicked and sinful men can prosper, if only because many of the ways of prospering are wicked and sinful, but as John Dod and Richard Cleaver (perhaps with Bayley and Baxter the most popular of the English Puritan casuists) affirmed, 'False dealing is no profitable trade to gain by, it rather hurteth than helpeth those that use it [for their] wealth will forsake them ... and God will curse them and poverty will oppress them' (Dod and Cleaver 1607, p. 63). We know, too, that sinners can be wealthy because some men use their wealth sinfully; and in some cases, or rather, in the case of some (not all) sins – such as debauchery, idleness and extravagance (precisely the sins of the 'Protestant ethic') – the sin is often self-punishing and likely to render the sinner's wealth short-lived. Dod and Cleaver again pointed this out: 'He that carrieth himself slothfully in the works of his calling ... is like to him that prodigally wasteth his substance ... and shall ... come to poverty ... The Holy Ghost condemneth them both to be sinful' (Dod and Cleaver 1611, p. 9). Arguments of this kind, then, help to resolve the apparent contradictions, and to restore, in the long run if not in the short, the correlation of godliness and worldly prosperity. But a correlation which works only in the long run makes it impossible to use one's prosperity as an index of one's state of grace: the answer it gives today could be contradicted tomorrow.

The argument of long-run correlation has another weakness: though less easily open to empirical refutation than the assertion of a correlation *tout court* , it can still be refuted by experience. Probably it matches reality no better. Further arguments were needed, and were provided, in the form of glosses on the 'promises of this life' which the godly are entitled to expect. One such was to explain (as was frequently done) that these promises do *not* mean that the godly should expect to be rich in a material sense during this life, but rather that they should expect to be happy and contented with their material circumstances. This implies they will have, in material terms, at least what is necessary, perhaps a modest degree of comfort, but not 'abundance'. Thus Perkins, answering the 'allegation' 'that God hath made a promise to every righteous man, that he shall receive abundance', explains that 'by riches in the word of God is often understood things necessary, and *not* abundance' (Perkins 1608, p. 746, emphasis added). The Scot James Durham agreed: the Biblical 'promise' that the godly man 'shall not want any good thing' means he shall have not 'riches ... but only what is convenient' (Durham 1676, p. 249). Many other Puritan and Calvinist spokesmen offered similar interpretations.[6] And after all, given the moral dangers attendant on wealth (described above), abundance may not be particularly desirable; but neither, on the other hand, is poverty, which, it was held, also carries with it temptations to sin. Thus a frequent theme is that the best condition is a medium one, between poverty and riches, and with that the godly Christian will be content. Discontent, that is, desire for more than one needs, is likely to be a manifestation of the sin of avarice or covetousness, and a sign of reprobation.[7]

Whether or not this argument is convincing, it still fails to solve the problem of empirical disproof. The most godly men and women might encounter total economic disaster, and for such people too the spokesmen of ascetic Protestantism had to provide a meaningful account of their condition. To do so, they offered an alternative gloss on the 'promises of this life'. This can hardly be better or more clearly stated than it was by the Scot William Colvill: 'All temporal promises are to be understood, with a secret clause of provision; if the performance of them shall be for the glory of God, and the spiritual benefit of his children' (Colvill 1673, p. 91). And not only could wealth be harmful to the latter, as we have seen, but also material poverty and deprivation could be beneficial. As Durham put it, 'God's trysting his people with wants, discovers his great wisdom, for he doth so, that they may learn to live by faith, ... and know the necessity of a humble dependence upon him' (Durham 1759, p. 321). God, says Perkins, may wish 'to exercise and try [the righteous man] by want and poverty' (Perkins 1608, p. 746), or, as Dod and Cleaver put it, 'lay poverty on his servants for a trial and exercise', in which case 'they have hope, and patience, and all inward supportance, which maketh the defect of outward things easy to them' (Dod and Cleaver 1606, p. 96). Thus they are enabled to demonstrate the steadfastness of their faith under God's 'crosses', and so assure themselves in the most convincing way of their election. No earthly benefit could be greater than this.

These arguments, if accepted, finally remove the contradictions between the promises and real life experience, but in effect do so by totally giving up the equation of prosperity and election that Weber claimed to detect. But there is yet another – a fourth – explanation of these matters to be found in the writings of the Puritans and Calvinists, indeed, of Calvin himself. 'To urge us [to obedience] by all possible motives', says Calvin, God 'promises also the blessings of the present life, as well as eternal felicity, to ... those who keep his commandments, the transgression of which he threatens not only with present calamities, but with the torments of eternal death' (Calvin 1813, Vol. I, p. 391). If then, as Calvin admits is the case, the elect suffer 'numerous and various calamities' (see above, p. 46), this is of small moment if God's promises have induced in them obedience to His will. There are two alternative reasons why the latter may be esteemed the supreme good: it may be a sign that the obedient are among the elect; or (if not) it may simply be pleasing to God.[8]

It is now time to sum up the significance of this part of the discussion. When, in the previous chapter, I argued that Weber over-simplified ascetic Protestant teachings about the work ethic, I did not in the least impugn that ethic's existence – rather, I argued that its relation to salvation and election was more complex and less consistent than Weber thought. I even suggested that this more complex and less consistent reality could well be a more powerful motivator of the work ethic than in Weber's own version. The present discussion may seem superficially similar, but its import is quite different. If, as Weber claimed, success in business was considered to be a sign of salvation or election, such a belief could plausibly be expected to motivate the pursuit of profit, of 'forever renewed profit' (Weber 1930, p. 17). If no such belief existed, there would be no such motivation. My argument has been that the belief in question, while not quite non-existent, existed far less than Weber claimed.

How damaging is this to the Weber Thesis? The answer is, not nearly so damaging as might be thought. The supposed correlation of worldly prosperity and eternal salvation is only one part of Weber's 'Protestant profit ethic': he also, and I think much more significantly, claimed that the ethic included an *explicit* injunction to pursue profit, by all honest means, as one of the obligations of the earthly calling. Such is the burden of the passage from Richard Baxter quoted above (p. 9). This is much more significant, because, in the first place, it is a much more surprising and unusual idea (whereas the idea of a correlation between success and virtue, in various versions, is, I have suggested, not unusual at all). To explain the singular historical development of Western industrial civilization, one needs something singular, not commonplace. And in addition, the notion of a requirement to earn as much profit as one (honestly) can corresponds much more closely to the essence of the spirit of capitalism, the concept of (as we now say) profit maximization. Although it has been much discussed, equation of success with salvation is something of a red herring. It is time to turn to the central issue: the idea of an obligation to devote oneself to profit-making.

Wealth, avarice and stewardship

What was the attitude of ascetic Protestantism to the pursuit of wealth? In a way that will by now be familiar, I shall argue that the answer given to this question in the Weber Thesis over-simplifies the historical reality. The truth is that powerful arguments both for and against wealth-seeking can be derived from the fundamental Protestant moral ideas. Once again, we should not expect the Calvinist and Puritan preachers to be unanimous on this subject, and they were not (though in this case individual spokesmen are less open to the charge of inconsistency). As is to be expected, different spokesmen weighted the opposed considerations differently, and resolved the issues in different ways. This remains true even if we restrict ourselves to the only kind of wealth-seeking that is relevant to the Weber Thesis, namely, pursuit of wealth in a lawful calling.

We already know, of course, that ascetic Protestantism had strong reasons to look with disfavour on material acquisition. Avarice, as we have seen, had always been considered by Christianity to be a grave sin, and continued to be so for Calvinists and Puritans. 'Beware of covetousness' said David Dickson, 'as of a special enemy to all true godliness' (Dickson 1651, p. 68). Another Scot, Andrew Gray, likewise warned against 'the idol of covetousness, and desire to the things of the world'; men must obey the injunction of the book of Proverbs, 'Labour not to be rich' (Gray 1839, pp. 177, 275). Other Biblical tags were frequently cited to similar effect: 'Lay not up for yourselves treasures upon earth'; 'Ye cannot serve God and Mammon'; 'The love of money is the root of all evil'. Lewis Bayley in his *Practice of Piety* was one of many Puritan divines to repeat a passage from Paul's Epistle to Timothy: 'They that will be rich, fall into temptation, and a snare, and into many foolish and hurtful lusts, which drown men in destruction and perdition' (Bayley, n.d., pp. 181-2).[9] And we know, already, what the divines meant by this. So many ways of acquiring wealth are sinful – cheating, dishonesty, oppression of the poor – that wealth-seeking is an activity liable to be perilous to the soul. And wealth, once acquired, even if lawfully, is a standing temptation to relax one's godly vigilance, and to fall prey to such sins as idleness, extravagance and debauchery. Successful wealth-seeking is perilous to the soul twice over.

William Perkins drew the moral in relation to the earthly calling. 'The end of a man's calling is *not* to gather riches ... but to serve God in serving of men, and in seeking the good of all men' (Perkins 1608-9, Vol. II, p. 146, emphasis added). 'They profane their lives and callings that employ them to get honours, pleasures, profits, worldly commodities, for thus we live to another end than God hath appointed, and thus we serve ourselves, and consequently neither God, nor men'. Of course, Perkins did not mean that a Christian, in the exercise of his calling, must be totally indifferent to earning a living: we must 'labour in our callings to maintain our families'. What he must not do, however, is to seek 'abundance': to do so is 'a hazard to the salvation of the soul'. 'Man may with good conscience desire and seek for goods necessary ... but he may not desire for goods more than necessary, for if he doth, he sinneth ...' (Perkins 1608, pp. 734, 769; Perkins 1609, Vol. II, p. 145).

Very similar views were expressed by John Preston. 'May not a man use his calling, to increase his wealth?' Preston asked, and answered 'that the end of men's callings is not to gather riches; but the end of our calling is to serve God and men'. A man may indeed 'care for his estate', but 'he must not aim at riches. God calls not a man to ... to seek excess, superfluity and abundance' (Preston 1641, pp. 254, 256-7). The Scot Samuel Rutherford expressed similar views: 'The desire [for food and raiment] simply is natural ... But the desire beyond measure ... , of that which is more than sufficient ... is the faulty desire, and ... is the sin' (Rutherford 1655, p. 270-1).

The attitude to wealth-seeking expressed by these views may be described as a wary realism. They were addressed to men working in the world, and their proponents had no intention of recommending withdrawal from that world. Some concern with material acquisition is therefore recognized as inevitable and indeed proper: what had to be resisted was the temptation to excessive acquisitiveness. But the realism of some of the Puritans went further: they recognized that diligence in a man's calling might well lead to prosperity, or, as they put it, God might well 'bless' or 'reward' their labours. In the words of Preston: 'If a man by diligence in his calling have riches following him, he may take them as a blessing of God bestowed on him, and as a reward for his calling'. But he was at pains to make a distinction: 'If riches come by your callings, that is the wages, not the end of our callings' (Preston 1641, p. 254). Riches may (by God's blessing) come to us: but they must not be *sought*.

We can now see that 'ascetic Protestant' attitudes to wealth-seeking (or rather, those surveyed so far) were quite complex: that is, it was held to be acceptable, but within specified limits and on certain conditions. It was, in fact, quite standard for Calvinist and Puritan moralists who discussed such matters (as many did), to compile lists of these limits and conditions. An example is James Durham: 'That one may lawfully increase his estate cannot be denied ... The great matter is to qualify it rightly 1. as to the end, 2. the measure, 3. the means, 4. the way and manner' (Durham 1676, p. 248). Durham went on to gloss these four conditions at considerable length, but in (over-simplified) summary, he meant that gain may be sought so long as this is done in a lawful calling ('the way and manner'), without deceit or dishonesty ('the means'), within necessary or moderate limits ('the measure'), and in the first place for the sake of God's glory and the good of our fellows, and for our own sakes only in order to provide what is necessary for ourselves, our family and our station ('the end'). We shall return later to this important matter of the right 'ends' in wealth-seeking.

These limitations were meant seriously and, where Calvinists and Puritans had the power to enforce them, they were enforced. Just as much as the medieval schoolmen, a Puritan such as William Perkins believed in the concept of the 'just price': whatever his attitude to profit, he would not tolerate profiteering. In a diatribe against 'hoarders up of corn' ('the vilest rascals in the land, ... cursed idolators, because [they] set [their] hearts upon riches'), Perkins' spokesman 'Christian' explains the root error of the profiteering 'worldling': 'it is thought no fault to raise the market, and to take for a man's own whatsoever he can get, and to sell at any price' – which is 'flat against the word of God' (Perkins 1609, Vol. III, p. 466). In other words, it is *not* permitted for the producer to take advantage of abnormally favourable market conditions, such as scarcity of supply. As with the schoolmen, the just price is the price set by a market in equilibrium. 'In all our traffic and bargains, as we would benefit ourselves, so must we benefit those with whom we deal' (Perkins 1609, Vol. III, p. 177).

The weight of Puritan influence, therefore, was against economic *laissez-faire* and in favour of price control. The society in which the Puritans exercised greatest power was undoubtedly seventeenth century New England – even in thoroughly Calvinistic Geneva and Scotland the clergy had to contend with the countervailing power of an entrenched and established magistracy, whereas, in New England, society and the state were a Puritan creation. There John Cotton, most influential of Puritan divines of the first generation, successfully sought for the official establishment of 'reasonable rates' for traded commodities. That such rates were enforced is shown by the famous case of Robert Keayne, the merchant of Boston, who was fined in 1639 for 'buying as cheaply as he could and selling for the highest price he could get' (Miller 1953, pp. 37, 48). Keayne, who considered himself to be a faithful and God-fearing Christian, was 'shocked' and 'amazed' – a circumstance which points to some discrepancy between Protestant and capitalist attitudes to profits. Other Puritan communities, less powerful than the New England clergy, took what action they could – for example Knappen reports the case of a tailor excommunicated by the Separatist congregation of Gainsborough because he charged an excessive price for doublet and hose (seven shillings instead of the 'just price' of five) (Knappen 1939, pp. 410-11).

It will be useful at this point to compare and contrast the attitudes to economic life and acquisition of the sixteenth and seventeenth century Puritans whom we have been discussing, and those of the pre-Reformation Christian moralists of the thirteenth to fifteenth century. In terms of James Durham's four conditions or 'qualifications' on wealth-seeking, no difference is discernable over two: 'the measure', and 'the means'. As to 'the way', there is a difference, namely the Puritan insistence that wealth must be sought only in a lawful calling – a concept which by now has been sufficiently discussed. What remains to be discussed, however, and is highly significant, is what Durham (and others) called 'the end', particularly the glory of God. The idea that one can seek wealth to the glory of God, as we shall see, makes a great difference.

What difference, exactly? If wealth-seeking can, so long as undertaken in the right spirit, be a means to glorify God, one might question whether there need *also* be any *quantitative* limit on it – what Durham called 'the measure'. And to be sure, the latter was sometimes omitted by Puritan writers who stressed that wealth must be sought only for the right reasons.[10] This is a departure from medieval attitudes, but it should be noted that it does *not* exemplify a Weberian profit ethic: it amounts to a (relatively) *permissive* attitude to wealth-seeking, but not a positive *injunction* thereto. If the Protestant profit ethic was permissive merely, then – while it might well have helped the development of modern Western capitalism – it would not have promoted it in the way asserted by the Weber Thesis. What, rather, would be implied would only be that Protestantism served to remove *obstacles* to capitalism created by traditional Christian views – a hypothesis more in conformity with the doctrine of Adam Smith in the *Wealth of Nations,* namely, that all that is needed for economic development is to maintain what he called 'the system of natural liberty', plus peace, the rule of law, security of property, and the avoidance of 'unnatural' political or religious obstructions. Smith's doctrine implies that, in such a setting, untrammelled 'human nature' – natural human propensities, ingenuity and self-interest – suffice for the continuing development of capitalism (Smith 1961, Vol. II, pp. 207-9). The Weber Thesis denies this, as we saw in the first chapter: in Weber's view, that development, in the manner we have actually experienced it in history, required in the first instance a specific and peculiar (and in his view, religious) *positive* sanction.

And of course, he asserted that the positive religious sanction for acquisition was indeed supplied – witness the words of Richard Baxter, for whom seizure of opportunities for honest profit is not simply permitted: it is a duty (to fail to do so is to 'cross one of the ends of your calling'). And this attitude becomes intelligible, if indeed wealth-seeking may be a way to glorify God. But what exactly does this mean? Baxter offers an explanation: 'If God show you a way in which you may lawfully get more than in another way (without wrong to your soul or any other), if you refuse this, and choose the less gainful way, you cross one of the ends of your calling, *and you refuse to be God's steward* ...' (Weber 1930, p. 162, emphasis added). To refuse to be God's steward is clearly, in Baxter's eyes, a sin. But to know exactly what he means by this, and hence to understand fully how it can be a religious duty to seize profit opportunities, we need to examine the idea of *stewardship* – a key concept about which Weber had surprisingly little to say.[11]

We can now begin to see why ascetic Protestant teachings on wealth-seeking are, as I suggested earlier, complex and contradictory. Up till now, I have stressed the religious grounds for extreme wariness, and even downright hostility, towards material acquisition, some of which even receive an added intensity from the Reformed version of Christianity, and especially from what I have called Weber's primary Protestant ethic. Wealth may lead one into sin, in the form of idleness, extravagance and debauchery. But the concept of stewardship reveals a different side of the question. Worldly wealth and goods, after all, are God's creatures, and the Protestants never doubted that they were created for use by men. The concept of stewardship means that they are entrusted to men by God, to be used in the right ways – in ways pleasing to Him. The good steward, then, is the man of wealth who uses his wealth rightly instead of allowing it to tempt him into sin. Possession of wealth, we now see, is not only a risk, but also an opportunity – an opportunity to use one's wealth in a godly fashion. Obviously, from this point of view, the wealthy man has a duty to act as God's steward, and the same is true if the wealth is acquired by diligence in an earthly calling. Such is the viewpoint of, for example, William Perkins, who (as we saw above) denied that one should use one's calling to *seek* wealth (or rather abundance). Perkins added, however, that 'If God give abundance, when we neither desire nor seek it, we may partake it, hold it and use it as God's stewards' (Perkins 1609, Vol. II, p. 146).

If we consider together the teachings of Perkins and Baxter, we can explain the difference between them as follows. Like every Puritan moralist who took it on himself to preach to laymen on the morality of wealth-seeking, they had to weigh up, on the one hand, the spiritual dangers inherent therein, on the other the virtues of stewardship to which it could be a means. Perkins gives weight to both, but gives more weight than Baxter to the dangers and less weight to stewardship than Baxter does. For Perkins one should not actively seek the responsibilities of stewardship, but leave such matters to God. For some writers, one *may* seek wealth, but, only on condition of using it rightly. Baxter, however, while not unmindful of the dangers involved, evidently takes the view that the Christian has the duty never to shirk the responsibilities of stewardship. The opportunity for lawful profit is, in effect, a call from God to assume the duties of stewardship in relation to that gainable profit: to shirk such a responsibility would be sinful. 'To choose the less gainful way' is to 'cross one of the ends of your calling' and to 'refuse to be God's steward'. In Baxter's eyes, one may say, the good Christian has a duty to maximize his stewardship-potential, as well as to actualize it.

Each of these Puritan solutions to the ethical dilemmas of wealth-seeking is understandable on religious grounds: none is ineluctably entailed by them. The dilemmas are scarcely to be avoided, just because stewardship is a fundamental, pervasive category in Puritan economic casuistry. The pages of the Puritan writers are peppered with the term, or if not the term the same idea is expressed by other words. It is an interesting question why this is so: I hazard the suggestion that the concept of stewardship is an aspect or analogue of what Weber called inner-worldly asceticism, and that the same general principles underly it as underly the doctrine of the earthly calling. According to the latter, men are creatures of God, created to serve His purposes and His purposes only: diligence in an earthly calling is the obligatory devotion of our persons, time and energy to these purposes.[12] It seems obvious that if we possess any usable property we must devote it too to God's purposes. This is the duty of stewardship.

Now, the duty of stewardship is an obligation incumbent on every possessor of wealth to use that wealth rightly, in accordance with God's will: it is not necessarily an obligation to *acquire* wealth, so that it can be thus used. For Baxter, however, it was so. An important question in relation to the Weber Thesis is how typical Baxter's interpretation is, in sixteenth and seventeenth century ascetic Protestantism. My impression, so far as England and Scotland are concerned, is that it was rather unusual, but by no means unique. In view of the importance of the issue in assessing Weber's argument I shall cite a few further examples of it. One is from Dod and Cleaver's *Plain and Familiar Exposition of the Ten Commandments,* in which these very widely read authors recommend 'frugality', which they explain refers to 'getting and keeping'. 'Our getting must be by some faithful labour in an honest calling' – of course. But also: 'God would have one labour in such a calling as should humble his flesh, pull down and tame his pride, and *bring some increase unto his outward estate,* so that he may have a merciful affection and also *ability to show mercy*' (Dod and Cleaver 1607, p. 322, emphases added). 'Of all men' say Dod and Cleaver in another place 'Christians be most provident to procure their own good prosperity' (Dod and Cleaver 1606, p. 31). Another example is provided by Samuel Rutherford: 'All the creatures of God in their own kind are good. But when we make any of the creatures an idol [they] are nothing else but vanity and vexation of spirit ... May we not, then, seek after the creature? Yes ... Seek the creature for God ...' (Rutherford 1885, p. 220). In the view of another Scottish divine, William Colvill, we 'should be diligent in seeking the good things of this world, because we are commanded of God to be diligent in our lawful callings' (Colvill 1673, pp. 72-3). According to John Cotton, the good Christian 'loseth no opportunity [to] bestir himself for profit – this will he do most diligently in his calling'. 'To see riches well got, and well employed' is pleasing to God who will probably reward this kind of rich man with 'spiritual gifts' (Cotton 1985, p. 31; Cotton 1641, p. 461).

For all of these writers, as for Baxter, wealth-seeking is a virtue, or even an obligation, but all (except Colvill) explicitly add the condition that it must be sought for the right reasons – for God, not oneself (Rutherford) – or in order to be put to the right uses – 'well employed', as Cotton says, or in Dod and Cleaver's words, to enable one 'to show mercy'. In other words, one should seek wealth in order to act as God's steward. Dod and Cleaver, also, tell us what, in large part, it means to be God's steward – it means to use one's wealth in works of charity. Baxter himself made the same point. It is not right, he points out, to think a man covetous just because he is 'laborious in [his] calling, and thrifty, and saving'; so long as he uses his gains 'for God, and charitable uses, there is no man taketh a righter course. He is the best servant for God, that will be laborious and sparing, that he may be able to do good' (Baxter 1673, p. 257). John Calvin himself explained the nature of stewardship in similar terms: 'Whatever God hath conferred on us, which enables us to assist our neighbour, we are the stewards of it, who must one day render our account of our stewardship' (Calvin 1813, Vol. II, p. 164). Innumerable similar passages explaining stewardship in terms of charity are to be found in the writings of the spokesmen of ascetic Protestantism.

It is time once again to take stock of the argument. This section has demonstrated that a Protestant profit ethic did exist, or, perhaps better, a Protestant profit-seeking ethic, and that its existence is understandable on religious grounds. But a Protestant anti-profit-seeking ethic also existed, and equally understandably. In relation to the Weber Thesis two problems arise. One is that the anti-profit-seeking ethic seems more typical and widespread; but there is another problem. The nature of the Protestant profit-seeking ethic that we have discovered seems to have a rather dubious relation to Weber's spirit of capitalism. In the spirit of capitalism, profit-seeking is the *summum bonum* and an end in itself; in the Protestant ethic, as we have found it so far, it is not an end in itself, but a means to enable godly men to do good works pleasing to God, above all works of charity for the needy. It might be doubted whether wealth-seeking undertaken in this spirit would promote capitalist economic development – rather, the wealth accumulated would continually tend to be withdrawn from economic production. In the next chapter, I shall consider these problems further by reviewing an important body of evidence which, up till now, seems to have been unaccountably neglected in discussions of the Weber Thesis. The question is whether this evidence yields a version of the Protestant profit-seeking ethic that might seem more directly supportive of capitalist behaviour, and whose influence might be widespread and significant.

5 The Westminster Assembly's Shorter Catechism and its sources

Anyone concerned to assess the Weber Thesis ought to pay careful attention to one particular form of literature that was the primary vehicle used by Protestants, and especially Puritans, for conveying to the laity the essence of Christian faith and doctrine, as they interpreted them – the catechism.[1] Strangely, this has not to my knowledge been done in any systematic way. Catechisms, whether official or unofficial, teach the religious essentials by formulating them in a series of questions and answers, and thus lend themselves not only to inculcation but to testing of the Christian's knowledge of his or her faith. The pioneer of Protestant catechizing was Luther himself, followed by Bullinger, Calvin, Beza, and many other leaders of Reformed Christianity. In England and Scotland, the countries arguably most relevant to the Weber Thesis and the focus of this study, literally hundreds of catechisms were written and published in the course of the sixteenth and seventeenth centuries. The first official catechism of the Church of England dates from Thomas Cranmer's famous Prayer Book of 1549. According to one authority (Ian Green), 280 known catechisms were published in England in the period 1549-1646 (a figure which is only the tip of a huge iceberg), while three-quarters of a million copies of *unofficial* catechisms are estimated to have been in circulation in England by the early seventeenth century, when the population was about four million (Green 1986, pp. 400, 425). The importance of catechisms, therefore, can scarcely be doubted. But the catechisms most important from the point of view of the Weber Thesis are, beyond question, the two adopted in 1647 by the Westminster Assembly of Divines, during the English (and Scottish) Civil War. In that war, most if not all English Puritans, and the Reformed Presbyterian Church of Scotland, were (at least up to 1647) supporters of the Parliamentary forces in their struggle against the Royalists. The anti-Royalist forces were, from the beginning of the war in 1642, in control of London; hence in 1643 the English Parliament was able to summon to Westminster an Assembly of 'learned and godly Divines', of both kingdoms, 'for the settling of the Government and liturgy of the Church of England', in a manner 'nearer agreement with the Church of Scotland, and other Reformed Churches abroad'. This momentous Assembly, which remained in session from 1643 until 1649, produced the famous Westminster Confession of Faith and two catechisms, a Larger and a Shorter. The catechisms had been approved by the English Parliament by 1648, and in the same year were adopted by the General Assembly of the Church of Scotland. In 1649 they were ratified by the Scottish Estates in Edinburgh (Mitchell 1883, p. 439).

The Westminster documents amount to an official summary of the essentials of British Calvinistic orthodoxy as of the mid-seventeenth century. The Confession of Faith is a theoretical statement, whereas the catechisms were, of course, designed for teaching. Of the two, however, it was the Shorter Catechism that was to be much the more influential, and most influential of all in Scotland (though not there alone by any means). As a Principal of Glasgow University, Sir Donald MacAlister summed up the relevant history early in this century, the Larger Catechism turned out to be 'for admiration rather than use', while the Shorter Catechism 'entered into the blood of Catholic Presbyterianism' (MacAlister 1925, p. 16). I mentioned in an earlier chapter that Scotland, an economic backwater at the time of its Reformation in 1560, was in the eighteenth and nineteenth centuries in the forefront of the Industrial Revolution. It is a tempting hypothesis that the Shorter Catechism played a not insignificant role in this transformation, as one of the major formative influences on the Scottish mentality in the intervening period.

That this was so depends on two fundamental facts – the official adoption of the Westminister Catechisms by the Church of Scotland, and the pivotal position of the Church in the life of the nation, including in particular the educational system, especially following the re-establishment of undiluted Presbyterianism in 1690 after the 'Glorious' Revolution. The Church of Scotland took catechizing very seriously indeed. Already in 1649, the General Assembly directed ministers and kirk sessions to ensure possession of both the Larger and Shorter Catechisms in every house 'where there is any one who can read'. In 1652, the Assembly enacted that part of the Shorter Catechism be explained in church to every congregation every Sunday, with individuals being publicly questioned thereon; ministers were also to make frequent visits to check that household heads were properly instructing their children and servants in the Catechism, and were to report the negligent to the kirk session. Doubtless, the Church did not achieve perfect success in this programme; but it had an effect. According to S.W. Carruthers, it was still common practice in late nineteenth century Scotland to study half of the Shorter Catechism in the family every Sunday evening (Carruthers 1957, pp. 7, 9).

Perhaps the most significant part of the Assembly's enactment of 1652 was that which directed ministers to ensure that the Catechism was taught in the schools, of which, from 1690, the Church had effective control. Even earlier, in 1649, the Assembly had ordered that the Shorter Catechism 'be printed severally with the ABC'; the intention being that it be used as the medium for teaching children to read (Carruthers 1957, p. 11). It was still in general use for this purpose in the eighteenth century.[2] Somewhat later, in 1794, the Assembly decreed that children be 'required to commit the [Shorter] Catechism to memory, and by frequent repetition to fix it deep into their minds' (Carruthers 1957, p. 7). Although the national Church suffered Disruption in 1843, the breakaway Free Church remained as passionately wedded to the Shorter Catechism as its parent; and, despite a gradual attenuation of the Church's legal position in education after 1860, memoirs of a number of distinguished Scots, such as the writer Neil Gunn,[3] and the artist James McBey, testify that the policy decreed by the Assembly in 1794 remained in vigorous operation at least to the end of the nineteenth century (McBey 1977, pp. 15-16).

In all of this there was, in a way, nothing unusual. The Church of England's Prayer Book Catechism was also taught to schoolchildren for centuries, and, bound with an ABC, was widely used as a first reading-book, at least for a time. So was another catechism that received official Church of England endorsement later in the sixteenth century, that of Alexander Nowell (Durbin 1987, pp. 6, 143; Hutchison 1984, p. 100). These facts undoubtedly have their importance, even if it is doubtful that the Church of England ever achieved or even attempted a rigour or comprehensiveness of indoctrination comparable to its Scottish counterpart. More importantly, in the present context, the Anglican Prayer Book catechism is a much briefer document than the Westminister Shorter Catechism, and (like Nowell's catechism) differs significantly from it in content – as will become apparent below.

If, as many believe, the Shorter Catechism has been such a powerful formative influence on the Scottish psyche, nevertheless it was not a Scottish creation, for the Westminster catechisms were almost entirely the work of English Puritan divines. Principal MacAlister enthusiastically summed up the relation in these words:

'The system of popular education initiated and fostered by John Knox and his successors gave the Scottish people a power of apprehension that enabled all classes to assimilate what the minds of the best Englishmen had prepared' (MacAlister 1925, p. 26). But, value judgments apart, it would be a mistake to suppose that the influence of the Shorter Catechism was confined to Scotland (Mitchell 1883, p. 433; Carruthers 1957, pp. 3, 6, 45). On the contrary, it was widely used and diffused among all English-speaking Presbyterians and other denominations of English Dissent. It was used by the Independents both in England (where they were a minority) and in New England (where they were dominant). In New England, the Shorter Catechism was used, as in Scotland, as a first reading-book, and may have been almost as important a formative influence there. Of considerable interest is the fact that the Catechism was also adopted, in a modified form, by Baptists and Wesleyan Methodists, whose theology is not (or not uniformly) Calvinist, but whose morality can be broadly described as Puritan. This parallels the point made by Weber about these denominations in his famous essay, illustrating how an ethic originally grown out of a Calvinistic theology could detach itself from these specific theological roots (Weber 1930, pp. 139-43, 146-51). In a sense, his whole thesis about the (secular) 'spirit of capitalism' is that it resulted from a similar process.

The eighth commandment

The diffusion of the Westminster Shorter Catechism, we have now seen, coincided more or less exactly with English-speaking 'ascetic Protestantism', as Weber called it. It is time now to consider its content, insofar as this is relevant to the Weber Thesis. The Catechism condenses the essentials of Christian faith and conduct into 107 questions and answers, occupying, in a recent edition, some sixteen pages (Free Church of Scotland 1973). Of the 107 answers some 49, including the first 40, set out the basic essentials of reformed Christian doctrine – on God and man, sin, redemption through Christ, effectual calling, justification, adoption, sanctification, faith, saving grace, election to eternal salvation. The remaining answers deal with three more detailed matters: the ten commandments (questions 41-81); the two sacraments, baptism and the Lord's Supper (questions 91-97); and the six petitions, preface and conclusion of the Lord's prayer (questions 99-107). In covering these topics the Catechism follows a quite orthodox catechetical pattern. The section of particular relevance, however, is that dealing with the ten commandments, and more especially the Decalogue's 'second Table', which prescribes duties of Christian conduct in the secular world. On each of these commandments, the Catechism asks and answers three questions: what the commandment is, what it requires, and what it forbids. There is, however, one commandment above all that is relevant to the Weber Thesis – the eighth. Here is what the Westminster Shorter Catechism contains on that subject:

Q. 73   Which is the eighth commandment?

A.   The eighth commandment is, *Thou shalt not steal.*

Q. 74   What is required in the eighth commandment?

A.   The eighth commandment requireth the lawful procuring and furthering the wealth and outward estate of ourselves and others.

Q. 75   What is forbidden in the eighth commandment?

A.   The eighth commandment forbiddeth whatsoever doth or may unjustly hinder our own or our neighbour's wealth or outward estate.

Some comments seem appropriate on these words, which constitute the sum total of what the Shorter Catechism has to say on the subject. In the first place, they strike the late twentieth century reader as a very surprising interpretation of the Old Testament injunction against stealing. If one examines, in particular, the Answer to Question 74, one finds that three things are being commanded: that one increase one's own wealth; that one increase the wealth of others; and that one do both in a lawful manner. Only the third of these (put as a mere qualification of the other two) seems to have much similarity to the usual idea of what not stealing means. The other two jointly enjoin material enrichment, or the promotion of economic prosperity. Most germane to the Weber thesis, the increase of one's own wealth is made a duty, just as much as that of others. It is hardly too much to say that this part of the Shorter Catechism turns the eighth commandment into a Protestant profit ethic. Most striking of all, this pursuit of material wealth is apparently prescribed without limit (though not of course unconditionally), as an end in itself – no ulterior end is mentioned. We seem to have here not only a profit ethic; not only a profit-seeking ethic; but a profit-seeking ethic totally congruent with Weber's 'spirit of capitalism'.

But if this is so, some major puzzles and questions remain. Why should the Westminster divines have identified not stealing, in part, with furthering one's wealth? And why in any case should they have considered furthering one's wealth to be a duty? How do their reasons for this relate to the considerations discussed in the previous chapter? The answers to these questions cannot be gleaned from the Shorter Catechism itself. It is therefore natural to turn for help to the rich history of earlier catechizing, especially Protestant catechizing.

Protestant Catechisms of the Sixteenth and Seventeenth Centuries

A survey of Protestant catechisms of the sixteenth and seventeenth centuries shows that the Westminster Shorter Catechism's 'Weberian' interpretation of the eighth commandment is quite unusual. As mentioned above both Luther and Calvin wrote catechisms. For Luther, as for Roman Catholics, the commandment 'Thou shalt not steal' was still the seventh commandment (the Protestant re-numbering came later). In his *Short Catechism* of 1529, Luther cites the commandment, and answers the question, 'What does that mean?' as follows:

> We are to fear and love God, that we take not our neighbour's money and goods, nor seek to obtain them by false dealing or deceit, but help him to keep and improve his goods and his sustenance (Luther 1896, p. 6).

Luther's *Greater Catechism* (1530) naturally goes into much greater detail, but does not mention any duty to further one's own wealth, or anything like it. Nor does Calvin's *Geneva Catechism* of 1541, a manual intermediate in length between Luther's two. Calvin has this to say:[4]

Minister   Go on to the eighth commandment.

Child   *Thou shalt not steal.*

M.   Doth this commandment forbid only such robberies as be punished by common laws, either doth it reach any further?

C.   This commandment reacheth unto all unlawful and deceivable occupations, whereby we pluck unto us any part of our neighbour's substance, whether it be by violence, by fraud, or by any other means which God hath not allowed by his word.

The next exchange between 'Minister' and 'Child' emphasizes that God's law forbids not only the sinful deed but also all 'purposes and the desires of our minds, to come by riches through our neighbours' loss'. Then comes the final exchange on the subject:

M.   What behoveth us then to do?

C.   We are bound to do our endeavour, that every man hath his due and right.

Calvin's successor at Geneva was Theodore Beza, who came to exercise great authority over the self-consciously 'reformed' churches. Beza was the author of two catechisms, called in English *A Little Catechism* and *A Book of Christian Questions and Answers*. Neither, however, contains any discussion of the commandments, and hence cannot have inspired the passage of interest in the Westminster Shorter Catechism. As for the catechisms of Luther and Calvin, two points are at once apparent. First, their interpretations of the commandment against stealing appear much more 'natural' than the Westminster interpretation – much more in accord with the normal meaning of the words. But secondly, even Luther and Calvin seem also to give the commandment a somewhat broader interpretation than might be expected. To Calvin, it implies that we must endeavour to ensure 'that every man have his due and right'; for Luther, that we must help our neighbour 'to keep and improve his goods'. This latter is quite close to the Shorter Catechism's duty to 'further the wealth of others'.

It is not difficult to explain this, however. Luther and Calvin were here following a principle which, well before 1647, had become standard, and is in fact made explicit in a number of catechisms written in English. Several such catechisms include, as well as (or sometimes instead of) discussion of individual commandments, sets of rules for the interpretation of the commandments generally. These rules are in all cases very similarly expressed. An example is Richard Greenham's *Brief and Necessary Catechism* of 1602, which lists four 'rules, which serve for the better understanding of every one of the commandments'.[5] The first rule is as follows:

In every commandment where evil is forbidden, the contrary good is commanded; and where any good duty is commanded, the contrary evil is forbidden.

Application of this principle to the sixth commandment (against murder) regularly yields the interpretation that we must not only abstain from unlawful killing, but also, as necessary, do what we can to preserve the life of others. Correspondingly, the eighth commandment, against stealing, will include the duty to help protect their goods, and generally uphold their property rights; as Calvin put it, ensure 'that every man have his due'. But there is also a difference between life and property: property can be not only preserved but increased. Hence Luther's formulation, that we must help our neighbour 'to keep *and improve* his goods', and the Shorter Catechism's duty to 'further the wealth of others'. None of this is directly relevant to the issue of the profit ethic, but it has an indirect relevance, as will appear below.

Calvin's Geneva Catechism was officially adopted for use by the Church of Scotland, one of several to be so authorized before 1648. The others were the Heidelberg Catechism of Ursinus and Olevianus published in 1563, John Craig's *Short Sum of the Whole Catechism* of 1581, and the so-called New Catechism of 1644 (Torrance 1959). All of these contain detailed consideration of the ten commandments; none interprets the eighth commandment as including a duty to increase one's own wealth. The New Catechism is of particular interest, having been adopted only four years before the Catechisms of Westminster, which superseded it – indeed, it was adopted while the Westminister Assembly was in session, apparently with the intention of influencing it. Here is what it has to say about the eighth commandment:

Q. 102   What is commanded in the eighth precept?

A.   To be content with the means of living which God gives us in a lawful way, and to help others as we are able in their necessity.

Q. 103   What is forbidden in it?

A.   All covetousness, whereby we unlawfully take our neighbour's goods and property, as by oppression or robbery, or under cover of the law, by theft, by false measures or false weights (Torrance 1959, pp. 175-6).

These answers, as can be seen, introduce a number of familiar themes relating to wealth-seeking. It will emerge that the interpretations of the New Catechism are much more representative of catechisms in general, than are those of the Shorter Catechism of the Westminster Assembly.

The Church of England has had fewer officially sanctioned catechisms than its Scottish counterpart. Cranmer's Prayer Book Catechism is relatively brief, and discusses the commandments of the second Table *en bloc* rather than individually (though it is possible to correlate specific commandments with at least some of the duties listed). These duties do not include any duty to further the wealth either of oneself or others. Alexander Nowell's *Catechism, or Institution of Christian Religion* received official endorsement from the Anglican Church in 1570, as a supplement to the Prayer Book Catechism, at a moment when the hierarchy was relatively friendly to the Church's Puritan wing. Its discussion of the eighth commandment is quite lengthy (too lengthy to quote) but again contains no duty to increase the wealth of self or others.[6]

The pre-1648 Puritan movement in the Church of England did not of course adopt any catechisms officially, but it did have recognised leaders who wrote catechisms. Thus Thomas Cartwright, the 'founder' of English Presbyterianism, is believed to be the author of a catechism called *A Treatise of Christian Religion* (by 'T.C.'). Likewise William Perkins produced a catechism called *The Foundation of Christian Religion Gathered Into Six Principles*; and a later Puritan leader, William Ames, one called *The Chief Heads of Divinity* (1612). All discuss the commandments; none mentions a duty to increase wealth, either of oneself or others. Perkins' discussion of the eighth commandment is very brief; that of Ames is longer and more interesting:

Quest.	What is the 8. Commandment?
An.	Thou shalt not steal.
Quest.	What is the scope of this commandment?
An.	For the maintenance of men's estate in the goods of this life.
Quest.	What is required?
An.	First that every man be exercised in an honest calling with diligence;
	2. That in that calling he live contented with his position;

| | 3. | That he useth that which God giveth him frugally for himself, and towards others with justice, liberality and mercy as occasion serveth. |

| Quest. | What is forbidden? |

An.	1.	All idle and unprofitable living;
	2.	Immoderate care of this world, and desire of gain;
	3.	All excess of sparing or spending;
	4.	All unjust dealing either by force or fraud;
	5.	All unkind and merciless dealing.

Three points are worth noting about this fragment of Ames' catechism. First, it illustrates a general point, that the more elaborated catechetical commentaries on the eighth commandment constitute, in effect, a sketch of a religious (in this case Puritan) economic ethic (the 'scope of the commandment' being, as Ames puts it, 'men's estate in the goods of this life'). Second, Ames' version of this economic ethic has many obvious affinities with the 'inner-worldly asceticism' of Weber's 'Protestant ethic' – for instance, the injunctions to 'be exercised in an honest calling with diligence', and to use material goods 'frugally'. Yet – thirdly - there is no sign of an 'ethic of profit', but rather, if anything, the reverse – 'immoderate desire of gain' is forbidden, and 'contentment with one's position' is enjoined (as by the 1644 Scottish New Catechism).

Not only is the Westminster Shorter Catechism crucially different from these authoritative predecessors: it differs likewise from the generality of contemporary and earlier catechisms – though not from all. To say just how exceptional it is would require a more comprehensive study than I have undertaken. I have, however, consulted 143 catechisms other than the Westminster Catechisms published before 1650,[7] of which 92 contain discussions of the ten commandments and 88 have commentary specifically on (or, in a few cases, relating to) the commandment against stealing. (These figures include a few works which are not strictly catechisms in the sense of following a question-and-answer format, but do contain instruction on the meaning and implications of the commandments.) Of the 88, six are Roman Catholic works (one is pre-Reformation),[8] while a small number (perhaps three) of the Protestant catechisms are expressions of what may be called a definitely 'anti-Puritan' position. Of the remainder, the great bulk can be described as more or less Puritan, or else are Protestant productions dating from the period before Puritanism became an issue. Catechisms were overwhelmingly a

Protestant/ Puritan instrument. None of the Catholic or anti-Puritan catechisms speak of a duty to increase one's wealth; but very few of the others do so either – on the most liberal interpretation, no more than ten.[9]

In short, we are faced with what by now is a familiar situation: a body of evidence, part of which seems to conform to the Weber Thesis, while some does not. In this case, however, a significant paradox is to be noted: on the one hand, the material supportive of Weber is, quantitatively speaking, only a small fraction of the whole; but on the other hand it appears to be *historically* much more important than the rest just because it includes the most influential authoritative formulation of 'ascetic Protestantism', the Westminster Assembly's Shorter Catechism. The Shorter Catechism is, in fact, the strongest argument in favour of the Weber Thesis that I know of. But how, we may wonder, did such an untypical doctrine as the Weberian interpretation of the eighth commandment come to be adopted as authoritative?

The sources of the Westminster Shorter Catechism's teachings on the eighth commandment

Fortunately for the student of the Weber Thesis, an investigation into the sources of the Wesminster Catechisms was undertaken some hundred or more years ago by Alexander Mitchell, a Moderator of the General Assembly of the Church of Scotland and Professor of Ecclesiastical History at the University of St Andrews (Mitchell 1886). It is largely thanks to Mitchell that something can be said by way of answer to the question that concludes the previous section.

The names of the divines who assembled at Westminster are known, and several of them, not surprisingly, were already authors of catechisms. I have read ten catechisms written by members of the Assembly, namely William Twisse, John White, Thomas Gataker, William Gouge, Henry Wilkinson, Thomas Wilson, George Walker, Herbert Palmer, William Good, and Samuel Rutherford, one of the Scottish Commissioners to the Assembly.[10] The catechisms of Gataker, Walker and Good are of no relevance, since they do not include discussion of the commandments. Of the remainder, three are of particular interest: those of Herbert Palmer, Samuel Rutherford, and Henry Wilkinson. It was to Palmer, already a well-known catechist, that the Assembly initially assigned responsibility for drafting its catechism, at first alone, later in conjunction with a committee of changing composition. After the Assembly's decision in early 1647 to prepare two catechisms instead of one, Palmer served for some time on the committee responsible for the Shorter Catechism. Rutherford, as one of the Scottish Commissioners, and thus entitled to serve on all the committees of the Assembly, participated in the committee on the Shorter Catechism.[11] Wilkinson did not serve on any of the committees concerned with the Westminster Catechisms, but of all the members of the Assembly he alone (so far as I know) was the author of a catechism whose interpretation of the eighth commandment at all resembles the Shorter Catechism's. Those of Twisse, White, Wilson and Gouge do not; more surprisingly, perhaps, neither do those of Palmer or Rutherford.

It is worth looking in a little detail at the catechetical formulations of some of these men. Gouge's *Short Catechism* (in its eighth edition by 1636) is short indeed on the point of interest – it states what is required by the eighth commandment in a one-word reply: 'Justice'. Twisse's *Brief Catechetical Exposition of Christian Doctrine* is not quite so brief; but in essence it reduces the eighth commandment to three injunctions: 'To labour in some lawful vocation'; 'Contentment with our estate'; and 'To help our neighbour in his estate' (Twisse 1633, pp. 44-5). White's, another popular catechism that by 1632 had reached its seventh edition, has the somewhat cumbersome title *A Plain and Familiar Exposition upon the Creed, X Commandments, Lord's Prayer and Sacraments, by Question and Answer*. His answers on the eighth commandment are extremely representative:

Q.   What doth the eighth Commandment require?

A.   The preservation of our neighbour's goods, justice in all our dealings, contentedness with our estate, frugality, and labour in an honest calling.

Q.   What doth it forbid?

A.   The greedy desire of riches, especially of other men's goods, idleness and unlawful callings, deceitful bargaining, oppression, the unlawful getting or withholding of any goods, public or private (White 1632, p. 18).[12]

The catechisms of Rutherford and Palmer should be of especial interest, since both were closely involved in the drafting of the Westminster Shorter Catechism. Neither, however, provides a source of the latter's treatment of the eighth Commandment. Rutherford's discussion of this issue is too long to quote fully, but the following extracts show that, broadly speaking, it resumes themes already familiar:

Q.   Quhat are we commandid in the 8 command?

A.   That we give to every man his own, be content with what God has given us, and labour for our living in a lawful calling...

Q.   Quhat are the special faultis in unjust conquesse?

A.   Theft, ... robbery and oppression ... extortion ... usury ... and deceit in buying or selling with false weightis, beguiling wares, and all unjust withdrawing of what is not ours ...

Q.   Quhat are the special virtues quherein we use our goodis right?

A.   In frugality or thriftiness, and liberality.

Q.   Quherein standeth thriftiness?

A.   In keeping carefully quhat God has given us, not wasting it either in gluttony, drunkenness, feeding the idle; ... or idleness, or negligence, or playing, or quhoring ...

Q.   Wherein standeth liberality?

A.   In an honest feeding and clothing of ourselves, and helping the necessities of the poor, and feeding the stranger ...

Q.   What is the special vice that this virtue fighteth against?

A.   Against that monster of many headis, covetousness and avarice, the root of all evil (Mitchell 1886, p. 238).

Here again we see much overlap with Weber's 'primary Protestant ethic' but no profit ethic. As for Palmer's catechism, for reasons that will shortly appear, it does not lend itself to extended direct quotation: but, in summary, it interprets the eighth commandment as having the general purpose of 'preserving of men's goods and estates in all safety'; hence it forbids wronging men in their estates, oppressing them, defrauding them, and 'forbear[ing] to help them, or further their good, when we may without special wrong to ourselves' (Palmer 1644, p. 28).

Palmer's catechism (entitled *An Endeavour of Making the Principles of Christian Religion ... plain and easy*) has an unusual format, in which each section consists of one principal and several subsidiary questions, the latter of which are all framed in such a way as to be answered either 'Yes' or 'No'. Possibly because of his attachment to this method, Palmer's catechetical proposals to the Westminster Assembly encountered considerable opposition. By the time the Shorter Catechism was finalized he was no longer a member of the drafting committee, which was, at the end, under the chairmanship of Anthony Tuckney, Principal of Emmanuel College, Cambridge (and later of St. John's) (Mitchell 1883, pp. 409-18, 426-7). Some commentators have attributed to Tuckney the main role in drafting the Shorter Catechism, and especially its section dealing with the ten commandments (for example, MacAlister 1925, p. 19). However, Tuckney was not himself a catechist – indeed, no works of his published in his lifetime are known. Tuckney's importance to the Shorter Catechism, therefore, seems to have been administrative rather than intellectual.

Where did Tuckney and his committee find the inspiration for their interpretation of the eighth commandment? One possibility is the catechism of their fellow-Assemblyman, Henry Wilkinson, which contains the following:

Q.   What is the eighth commandment?

A.   Thou shalt not steal.

Q.   What is the end and drift of this commandment?

A.   That we should not impair our own or our neighbour's estate, but as far as we can procure the good of both (Wilkinson 1629, unnumbered pages).

However, although in meaning this seems to be close to the Shorter Catechism, it is not particularly close in wording – other catechisms, as we shall see, are closer. What is more, Wilkinson's catechism, unlike the Shorter Catechism, goes on to condemn (*inter alia*) covetousness, false dealing, and usury, and to enjoin contentedness with our estate and mercifulness to the needy (as well as diligent labour in a calling, and frugality). Although Wilkinson was a well-known catechist, he was by the time of the Westminster Assembly very old (born in 1566, he is described by Alexander Mitchell as probably its oldest member) (Mitchell 1886, p. xlviii). This may help to explain why he was not placed on any of the Assembly's catechetical committees, and may also have limited his capacity actively to influence his colleagues.

According to Mitchell, the most important direct source of the theology of the Westminster Assembly's catechisms, and of its Confession of Faith, is the writings of James Ussher, Archbishop of Armagh (Mitchell 1886, pp. xviii, xliv). It may seem to some surprising to attribute such an influence on the conclusions of Puritan divines to a leading Bishop of the established church. However, it is necessary here to bear in mind the differing, and overlapping, criteria of Puritanism. Anti-Episcopalianism is only one of these, and not the most important. So far as fundamental theology is concerned, Ussher (like many earlier Church of England bishops) was at one with the Calvinist system – indeed, he was one of its most distinguished exponents. As Mitchell puts it, in the doctrinal articles he compiled for the first Irish Convocation in 1615, Ussher 'sets forth with great distinctness those views of the Divine decrees so lucidly propounded by Augustine and Calvin'. In view of the great esteem in which his theological writings were held in Puritan circles, it is not surprising that he was invited to participate in the Westminster Assembly. However he declined – for political reasons.[13] This succession of circumstances indicates his position rather clearly.

Thus deprived of Ussher's personal presence and counsel, it would not be surprising if the divines of Westminster looked instead to his published works. Indeed, while the Assembly was in session Ussher published a catechism (which, he says, he had composed much earlier), called *Principles of Christian Religion* (1644). The treatment of the eighth commandment in this work is quite unlike that of the Westminster Shorter Catechism. The commandment, it says, 'concerneth the goods of this life; in regard either of ourselves, or of our neighbours'. In regard of ourselves, it commands that 'we labour diligently in an honest and profitable [i.e. useful] calling; content ourselves with the goods well gotten, and with liberality employ them to good uses'; in regard of our neighbours, 'that we use just dealing unto them ... , and use all good means that may tend to the furtherance of their estate' (Mitchell 1886, p. 147). In other words, as for Luther, we are commanded to further our neighbour's estate, but not our own.

Ussher, however, is also the author of another work, *A Body of Divinity* (1645) which may be called a catechism by virtue of its question-and-answer format, though it is so long that it could not have been intended for the instruction of ordinary Christians. Its explication of the eighth commandment alone covers twenty pages. But it does include, among much else, wording very reminiscent of the Westminster Shorter Catechism:

What are the words of the eighth Commandment?

Thou shalt not steal.

What doth it contain?

A charge of our own and our neighbour's goods: that we show love and faithfulness therein, and not only not impeach or hinder, but by all means preserve and further the same ...

What is forbidden in this Commandment?

Whatsoever is prejudicial to our own or our neighbour's wealth ...

What is required?

Whatsoever may further and prosper our own or our neighbour's wealth...by all lawful courses and honest dealing (Ussher 1648, p. 285).

One may speculate on the reasons for the different formulations adopted by Ussher in his two works. One is suggested by Mitchell. *The Body of Divinity* is avowedly 'collected out of sundry authors', and, says Mitchell, unlike the *Principles of Christian Religion* seems not to have been 'owned' by Ussher as an expression of his personal views – rather it was a compilation of the writings of other, reputedly orthodox divines (Mitchell 1886, p. xlv). If this is right, the source of the Westminster Shorter Catechism's treatment of the eighth commandment is, in a sense, still to seek. Which, 'orthodox divines' (or divine) served as source for Ussher and for the Westminster Assembly?

One can try to answer this question only by seeking similarities of wording. Of all the catechisms I have seen, two stand out as closest to the Westminster Shorter Catechism. One is by 'M.N.' (Mitchell 1883, p. 499),[14] at first thought by Mitchell to be probably Matthew Newcomen, an important Presbyterian divine who was present at Westminster, but now known to be Martin Nichols (or Nicholes, or Nicolls),[15] who was not. Nichols' catechism contains the following:

Q.   What is the eighth Commandment?

A.   Thou shalt not steal.

Q.   What doth this Commandment aim at?

A.   The preservation of men's outward estates.

Q.	What is required of us herein?
A.	That we do what in us lieth by all good and lawful means, to further the wealth or outward estate of our selves and others ...
Q.	What is the evil contrary hereunto?
A.	Any neglect to further, together with the doing or endeavouring to do any thing that may hinder or impair the outward estate of ourselves or others (Mitchell 1886, p. 131).

In one way, however, Nichols' catechism is unlike the Westminster Shorter Catechism in that its discussion of the eighth commandment contains much more than the above, including many of the elements we have noted in other catechisms. From the point of view of 'negative' as well as 'positive' similarity, the author providing the closest model for the Westminster Shorter Catechism is John Ball, who was minister at Whitmore in Staffordshire.[16] Ball's *Short Catechism* has the following:

Q.	What is the eighth Commandment?
A.	Thou shalt not steal.
Q.	What is the general duty of this Commandment?
A.	That by all good means we further the outward estate of ourselves, and of our neighbours.
Q.	What is the general sin forbidden?
A.	All neglect to further our own or our neighbour's wealth, all impeachment or hindrance thereof, and all increase thereof by unjust and indirect dealing (Mitchell 1886, p. 86).

That is all Ball's *Short Catechism* has to say on the eighth commandment. Its similarity to the Westminster Shorter Catechism is marked, although even Ball's answers are much more explicit than the other in forbidding enrichment by unjust means.

Of those two catechists, Martin Nichols and John Ball, little is known about Nichols, while Ball, who died in 1640, was in his day a well-known figure and author. His catechism, indeed, was extraordinarily popular – perhaps the most popular of all 'unofficial' catechisms. By 1645, it had reached its twenty-third edition, and was in its fifty-sixth edition in 1678.[17] It is interesting that Ball and

Nichols seem to have been close associates – indeed, some editions of Ball's *Short Catechism* are ascribed to Ball and Nichols jointly.[18] According to Brook's *Lives of the Puritans* 'Messrs Ball, Nichols ... and others' formed a group of divines who, after being harassed and ejected from their ministry during Archbishop Laud's ascendancy, were enabled to continue preaching by the patronage and protection of Lady Bromley of Sherriff-Hales in Shropshire (Brook 1813, p. 441). Ball was also the author of some admired longer works, notably *A Treatise of Faith*, and *A Treatise of the Covenant of Grace*, which was published posthumously in 1645. Alexander Mitchell notes that the latter has a preface by some prominent Westminster divines, which shows their knowledge of, and esteem for, Ball's catechism (Mitchell 1886, p. xlii).

In sum: the Westminster Shorter Catechism's interpretation of the eighth commandment, according to which the injunction not to steal implies a duty to further one's own wealth, while unusual, does have precedents, notably in the *Short Catechism* of Ball. Just why the Westminster Assembly chose to 'canonize' this unusual interpretation is a question probably impossible to answer. But it is possible to tackle another question. How did this relatively unusual (and at first sight surprising) interpretation of the eighth commandment arise at all? How does it fit into the framework of Protestant moral theology? Indeed, the first of these questions has already been answered in part – the eighth commandment was standardly glossed as a summary of Christian economic morality, and expanded as such. But we still want to know, if possible, why the authors of the Shorter Catechism *might* see their formulations as a succinct summary of that morality.

The Second Table of the Decalogue

For many centuries, the Decalogue (or Ten Commandments) has been conventionally divided into two Tables, with the first Table, according to the counting scheme early established by Protestantism, comprising the first four commandments, and the second Table the remaining six. The distinction is as follows: the first Table prescribes our duties to God, while the second Table prescribes our duties to men, or to our neighbour. Often the latter were summed up (by catechists and others) in a single phrase: 'to love our neighbour as ourself'. The commandment against stealing of course belongs to the second Table, which provides, therefore, a relevant context for the present enquiry. Nor is it the case (as has sometimes been suggested)[19] that catechists generally attached less importance to the second Table than to the first. True, some of them did assert the primacy of the first Table, but this priority was philosophical, not practical: it signalled a relation, not of more important to less important, but of premise to the conclusion entailed by it. In other words, our duties to our neighbour *follow* from our duty to God because God has commanded the love of our neighbour. Thus John Mico in his *Meat for the Stronger, or a Catechism for the Elder Sort*:

Q.   Why are the duties towards God set down before the duties to our neighbour?

A.   Because the love of God is the ground of our love of our neighbour...The love of our neighbour is the proof of our love towards God (Mico 1631, p. 46).[20]

In this sense, the duties of the second Table are duties towards God also.

It was not uncommon for catechists to consider the commandments of the second Table together as a group (instead of, or as well as, separately). In this case, it was usual to differentiate the tenth commandment (against *coveting* 'any thing that is thy neighbour's') from the rest, as forbidding sinful *desires*, as distinct from sinful acts of commission or omission, dealt with in commandments five through nine. Thus Samuel Austin, in his *Practical Catechism*, could sum up the latter group of commandments as requiring the love of our neighbours in regard to, respectively, their 'honours', their 'lives', their 'chastities', their 'estates', and their 'credits and good names' (Austin 1647, p. 15).[21] There is nothing very surprising about this (with the possible exception of the extension of the fifth commandment – 'honour thy father and thy mother' – to apply to all our neighbours, or at least all 'honourable' ones). What is more surprising, and more interesting, is that several catechists, as will be shown below, summed up the duties of the second Table in a significantly different way.

One catechism which offered a more elaborate account of the second Table was that of the Huguenot Matthew Virell, translated into English as *A Learned And Excellent Treatise containing all the principal grounds of Christian Religion*. According to Virell, the second Table 'prescribeth a holy policy or government among men, that they may keep peace among themselves, and serve God with united minds'. This requires, firstly, 'that some be superior and some inferior' – which is the burden of the fifth commandment. The maintenance of human society naturally requires 'that the life of man be preserved' – hence the sixth commandment. But man is mortal, hence 'in the seventh commandment, forbidding whoredom, [God] enjoineth marriage' and procreation therein. Since the sustaining of a family requires 'riches', the eighth commandment 'appointeth to every one property of goods', and 'quiet possession' thereof. However, possession of goods by sinful men tends to give rise to 'strifes and controversies, which the Magistrates cannot appease, except they do plainly know the truth of the matter' – hence the ninth commandment against bearing false witness (Virell 1594, pp. 132-3). Thus the circle of 'holy policy or government' is complete. Virell presents this group of commandments as a set of norms necessary to enable men to live together and serve God. Thus Virell can say that the commandments of the second Table ought to be kept, 'not indeed for our neighbour's sake, but for God's sake, of whom they be commanded' (Virell 1594, p. 79).

This perspective on the second Table is subtly different from Mico's (see above), and perhaps explains a way of understanding its injunctions which is significantly different from that of Samuel Austin. Our obligation is not so much to help others, as to enable all men to serve God – including ourselves. So far as these duties are concerned, all men – self and others – are from this point of view on an equal footing. Accordingly, Ezekiel Rogers, in his *Chief Grounds of Christian Religion set down by way of Catechizing*, summarized the second Table thus: 'That we maintain our neighbours' *and our own* dignity, life, chastity, goods, good name ...' (Mitchell 1886, p. 62, emphasis added). He was by no means alone in adopting such a formula. And it is interesting that several writers alternated (or equivocated) between this formula and a more strictly other-regarding one. Thus George Webbe's *Brief Exposition of the Principles of Christian Religion* (1612):

Q.   What do the commandments of the second Table teach us?

A.   Our duty towards our neighbour.

Q.   What is the sum of our duty towards our neighbour?

A.   We must love our neighbour as ourself ... and endeavour to preserve (as much as in us lieth) the persons, chastity, goods and good name, both of ourselves and others.

Chastity apart (which is obviously in a separate category, and relatively unproblematic) why should we endeavour to preserve our own persons, goods and good name (or credit)? The answer, presumably, is so that we can serve God, or serve Him better. In the case of our persons (lives) and our goods, there is another factor: these are God's creatures, given to men by God specifically for the furthering of God's purposes, as a kind of trust, rather than an outright gift. Hence the familiar Christian idea that suicide is a sin, and, in the explicit view of many of the catechists, a sin against the sixth commandment ('Thou shalt not murder'). So far as goods are concerned, the corresponding sin is waste, prodigal misuse of property, undue 'lavishness', and so on – and the opposite virtue is thrift, frugality and generally the preservation of one's estate. Injunctions to these virtues and against the opposite sin, in interpretations of the eighth commandment, are perhaps not so frequent as injunctions against killing or harming oneself in interpretations of the sixth – nevertheless, they are quite frequent. Out of my 88 sources (see above), some 24 include formulations of this sort in their explications of the injunction not to steal.

And with this, we have made contact again with Weber's 'Protestant ethic' or more precisely with what I have called its 'ethic of puritanism'. The thriftless man who wastes his property is usually seen also as an offender against this ethic – through riotous living, unnecessary luxury of apparel, gaming, whoring, and so on. But he offends also in another way: he fails to use God's gifts rightly, as a good steward, and it is in this way that he becomes an offender against the eighth commandment. For God has given us property for specific purposes, which include our own maintenance and that of our family, and also – very importantly – the relief of the needy through charity. Of my 88 sources, some 39 (a very high proportion) mention the duty of charity to the poor and needy as part of their interpretation of the eighth commandment.[22] The thriftless wastrel, who becomes unable to discharge this duty, steals from the poor, as well as from his wife and children. As the Huguenot Virell put it, 'we be commanded to deal with our neighbour according to charity, seeing that God has given us goods, to be stewards of them, to use them ourselves, so far as necessity requires, and to help the poor and needy. But whosoever keepeth not this rule, he conveyeth to himself other men's goods' (Virell 1594, p. 150).

Virell, however, added a qualification to this precept of charity. Our goods, he wrote, are 'for the poor, that by their own labour are not able to help their necessity. For they that be able by labour to sustain their life, and in the meantime become poor by idleness and sloth, be altogether unworthy to be relieved. For the Apostle commandeth; if any will not work, let him not eat'. In thus explicitly qualifying the duty of charity, Virell is exceptional among catechists; but he is the reverse of exceptional in embracing the principle which grounds his qualification, which is, of course, none other than Weber's famous 'work ethic' (the positive half of his 'primary Protestant ethic'). Indeed, in catechetical explications of the eighth commandment, no precept is more frequent than the injunction to diligence and industry in earthly work, avoidance of sloth and idleness, and so on. Out of my 88 cases, some 50 include exhortations of this kind,[23] and of these, over 30 explicitly place this duty in the context of the 'calling'. The duty to work in an earthly calling is absolutely characteristic of catechetical interpretations of the eighth commandment.

Why exactly is this so? As in the case of frugality and thrift, it is possible to distinguish the strictly ascetic ground for hard work (as 'mortification') from its status as a duty required by the eighth commandment. Weber remarked, in his famous essay, that for Luther labour in an earthly calling was, *inter alia*, 'the outward expression of brotherly love' – in it one plays one's part in a division of labour whereby each serves the rest (Weber 1930, p. 81). This idea is echoed by a number of catechists, who emphasize that one's calling must be useful or 'profitable' to society or the commonwealth (for example, Wilson 1620, pp. 251, 368; Dent 1601, p. 192). From this point of view, it is not hard to see how idleness offends against the eighth commandment – it robs one's fellows of the contribution to which they are entitled. But there is more to it than this. Let us recall Virell's scheme of 'holy policy or government among men', which requires, among other things, that the life of men be preserved, and perpetuated by means of the family. Hence, once again, the obligation to labour, in order to maintain oneself and one's family – as Virell himself pointed out (Virell 1594, p. 133). He was far from being alone in this: some seventeen (out of 88) catechisms inculcate a duty to labour 'to get one's living', or some such formula – including the Church of England's Prayer Book Catechism. Again, it is not hard to see how failure to live up to this obligation, thus becoming a burden on others, could be viewed as a form of theft. The anonymous author of *A Form of Catechizing in True Religion* (1581) put the point graphically:

> They that have no good trade to get their living by, but live idly on that which is others', not endeavouring to apply the strength which the Lord hath given

them, to some good means, which the Lord hath allowed men to use, they cannot assure themselves that they live by the Lord, and therefore are guilty of theft by this [eighth] commandment (p. 50).

Archbishop Ussher, in his *Body of Divinity*, likewise states that 'they that have no calling', those 'who can work and will not, but live upon other men's labours', are 'unprofitable burdens to the Commonwealth, and like pernicious humours to the body' (Ussher 1645, p. 293). They rob it of its substance.

But there is still more to it. The obligation to work, in order to maintain oneself and one's family, requires one to make (in a market economy) a certain amount of money – a strictly limited amount, given the 'ethic of puritanism'. Is there any reason, religiously speaking, why one should earn more? According to many catechists, there is – because of the duty of charity. About a dozen (out of the 88) explain that one reason for the imperative of diligence is to enable us to help the needy, or more generally, to help others (presumably, when necessary). Among the dozen are some very popular and important examples, such as Edward Dering's *Short Catechism for Householders*[24] and Stephen Denison's *Compendious Catechism*. The latter, which by 1632 was in its seventh edition, puts it thus:

> The eighth Commandment is this: Thou shalt not steal. Whereby I am taught ... to labour diligently in a lawful calling, that I may honestly maintain myself and them that belong unto me: yea, that I may be able to do good unto others that stand in need of my help (Denison 1632, p. 40).

The most extended and eloquent development of this theme that I have encountered is in John Paget's[25] *Primer of Christian Religion*, a lengthy and remarkable work which can be considered to be a catechism by virtue of its use of the question-and-answer formula. Paget's method is to invoke, in succession, every imaginable type of creature, ranging from the angels to the insects, in order to draw moral lessons relevant to the commandments. As for the eighth commandment, Paget's continually repeated theme is that its 'principal virtue' is 'to profit our brethren'. Here is how, according to Paget, the angels teach us this commandment:

> The food of the Israelites in the wilderness was called angels' bread, ... not because they did use to eat it, but because God did distribute it by them. They were God's ... stewards, to bestow and dispose his blessings. It is then an angelical office to distribute, and to communicate to them that want ... The Angels also appear unto men, in the place where they exercise the works of

their calling, as unto Gideon under the oak where he threshed, to Manoa's wife in the field, and to David in the threshing place of Araunah, teaching us to avoid idleness, and to be diligent in the work of our calling, so that we may get something wherewith we may profit our brethren (Paget 1601, pp. 5-6).

Paget continues, with much ingenuity and impressive literary skill, to show how the same lesson is taught by (among others) the cherubims, the seraphims, the sky and firmament, the stars, the bees, the pismires (or ants), the trees, the metals and the waters. Here is how the waters teach us to obey the eighth commandment, and to 'profit our brethren':

All the rivers run into the sea, yet the sea is not full ... Though ten thousand mighty rivers run every day into the sea, yet it is not one drop the fuller, because they are conveyed out as fast as they came in, partly by the Sun, that draws them into the clouds, and partly by the channels and conduits under the earth ... We are to ... follow [this] pattern that God hath laid before us; when rivers of wealth flow in, we are to send it out as fast as it comes, and to be never a whit the fuller, or the richer at the year's end (Paget 1601, p. 164).

This striking passage does not actually say that the more wealth one acquires, the better one will be able to help others. But such an inference could very easily be drawn. There is one place where Paget himself seems to draw it, namely, when he explains how the bees teach us to 'profit our brethren':

The Bees in their business are exceedingly diligent that their labours may profit, and the witness of their little bodies enduring great labour shall strike our strongest bones in pieces, if we labour not with them to profit ourselves and others (Paget 1601, p. 93).

It seems likely from this passage, taken in the context of Paget's total argument, that he sees diligence in profiting ourselves as a means to profiting others, the 'principal virtue' of the eighth commandment. Nevertheless, the last phrase quoted above – 'to profit ourselves and others' – is quite reminiscent of the phraseology of the Westminster Shorter Catechism.

The Westminster Shorter Catechism's teaching on the eighth commandment reconsidered

In view of all the evidence by now reviewed, it seems highly likely that the idea in the minds of the men who drew up the Westminster Shorter Catechism was similar to that expressed by Richard Baxter in the famous passage from the *Christian Directory*, and by a few other ascetic Protestant writers mentioned in the previous chapter: 'wealth and outward estate' are creatures of God bestowed on men as means which should be used for godly ends, hence a good Christian must not only preserve his wealth through frugality and thrift, but increase it by diligence in his calling, and by every just and honest means. Interestingly, perhaps, we know that Baxter warmly admired the Westminster Shorter Catechism, of which he spoke in the following enthusiastic terms: 'I do heartily approve of the Shorter Catechism of the Assembly and of all therein contained, and I take it for the best catechism that ever yet I saw' (Mitchell 1886, p. xxvi). Conceivably he may have been influenced by it. But Baxter himself, as we know, unlike the Shorter Catechism, enjoined wealth-seeking explicitly in the context of stewardship, meaning above all duties of charity. Several of the catechists who have been discussed are explicit in linking these ideas – two examples, already cited, are Paget and Virell. Another is Archbishop Ussher, who wrote that 'we are not absolute owners of the things that we possess: but God's stewards who are enjoined to employ his talents to such uses as he requireth; and particularly to the benefit of our fellow-servants' (Ussher 1645, p. 287).

Why is nothing of this to be found in the Westminster Shorter Catechism? Did its authors for some reason suppose that their interpretation of the eighth commandment as an injunction to increase one's wealth would be understood in terms of the duties of stewardship? However that may be, this injunction represents, in terms of religious ethics, what may be called a high-risk strategy. The same is true, perhaps to a lesser extent, of Baxter's injunction to choose 'the more gainful way'. It is safe to assume that neither of these injunctions was intended as an endorsement of self-interested acquisitiveness (avarice). But nor are they simply an instruction in how to be godly: rather, they make sense only on the assumption that the person who is their target is *already* a godly person. Their rationale is to show how the godly person is enabled to do godly works. In the case of writers such as Wilkinson, Ussher, Virell and Paget, who used similar formulae, all this is made sufficiently clear by the context in which the formulae are placed, discussed above, as well as by continual warnings (typical of the catechetical exegeses of the eighth commandment) against covetousness, inordinate desire of earthly goods, unfair methods of trading, and so on. The same is true even of the two catechists closest to the Westminster Shorter Catechism in their interpretations of the eighth commandment, Martin

Nichols and John Ball. Thus Nichols' *Catechism*, after telling Christians that they should further their 'outward estate' by 'labouring faithfully' in a 'lawful calling', goes on to instruct them that they must use that estate 'charitably' as well as frugally, dealing 'liberally' with their neighbours, 'as occasion requireth' (though not in the case of 'idlers' and 'wandering beggars') (Mitchell 1886, p. 131). As for John Ball, the writer whom I described earlier as exhibiting the greatest similarity, both positive and negative, to the Westminster Shorter Catechism, that description is true, but with a qualification. In addition to his *Short Catechism* (quoted above), Ball also published an expanded version, called *A Short Treatise Containing all the Principal Grounds of Christian Religion*, which is simply his *Short Catechism* with an additional 'Exposition' tacked on to the answers. On the eighth commandment, the added 'Exposition' enjoins *inter alia* 'true and honest dealing', 'contentation with our estate, be we never so poor' and 'giving freely ... according to our ability ... and our neighbour's necessity', and warns against the sin of covetousness (Ball 1631, p. 205) – all elements that are missing from his *Short Catechism*, and from the Westminster Shorter Catechism. If the point of increasing our wealth is to enable us the better to help others (and otherwise further godly projects) that is not made explicit in these two short catechisms. They do not, apparently, make self-enrichment conditional on godly use of the riches, but seem to endorse it as an end in itself.

Finally, it is worth considering, from this point of view, the Westminster Assembly's Larger Catechism, which up to now I have largely neglected. The Larger Catechism's discussion of the eighth commandment is both like and unlike that of the Shorter Catechism. It too enjoins the Christian 'by all just and lawful means, to procure, preserve and further the wealth and outward estate of others, as well as our own'. But it enjoins much else besides, including diligence in a lawful calling, frugality, 'giving and lending freely, according to our abilities and the necessities of others', and 'moderation of our ... affections ... concerning worldly goods'. At the very least, this is a more complex interpretation of the eighth commandment, a more complex economic ethic, than is to be found in the Shorter Catechism. But it was the Shorter Catechism, not the Larger, that was taught to generations of young Protestants in English-speaking countries. By boiling down that ethic to the bare formulae that have been quoted, the authors of the Shorter Catechism may have contributed, however unintentionally, to the secularization of the 'Protestant ethic' into the 'spirit of capitalism'. Could this be, in part, why J.A. Froude, the

English historian, found the Scottish character to be, in 1865, that of a people eminently religious, but characterized at the same time by 'long-headed, thrifty industry', as well as a 'sound hatred' of all waste and extravagance (Froude 1865, p. 27)?

6 The Spirit of Capitalism and the Protestant Ethic

If the discussion of the previous chapter has any merit, it suggests that Weber may after all have been right, in a sense, to suggest that ascetic Protestantism *unintentionally* promoted the spirit of capitalism; that is, motivated as an end in itself behaviour – namely, profit-seeking – which, according to religious ideas, should have served only as a means to other, godly ends. The present chapter will have two connected themes: the relation and, not infrequently, the confusion between ends and means in discussions of economic activity by spokesmen both of religion and of business, and the definition of godly uses of wealth, or in other words, of stewardship.

The idea of an ethic of investment

I argued in a previous chapter that the doctrine of stewardship and the doctrine of the particular earthly calling are closely analogous: both derive from the fundamental Protestant idea that all God's creatures, human and non-human, have been created by Him in order to serve His purposes, and must therefore be devoted to these purposes and these purposes only. Richard Baxter, as we saw, closely juxtaposed the two ideas of calling and stewardship, and proclaimed that the former is, in part, a means to the latter (that is, the calling is to be used to acquire 'stewardable' wealth). But, does not the reverse relation also hold? Should stewardship not serve the calling, as well as vice versa? The idea seems logical and attractive, in ascetic Protestant terms. After all, diligent activity in one's calling is behaviour pleasing to God: in this way we serve God by serving men, as Perkins put it. Surely, therefore, godly use of wealth must include using it to further and improve the practice of one's calling – in other words, investing it in one's business. And if one's calling is service to men as well as to God, it must be our duty to perform this service as well as possible, by the best methods possible. It is thus a Christian duty to be alert for opportunities to improve production methods, and to undertake the necessary investment. This very natural inference from Protestant doctrines could obviously be of great importance for capitalist economic development (and it would counteract the tendency for stewardship understood simply as charity to drain resources from economic enterprise); but it is clearly not Weber's spirit of capitalism. In fact, theoretically speaking, it reverses the relation between profit and investment that the latter would postulate – instead of investing for the sake of profit, the godly businessman would seek profit for the sake of further investment, and better performance of his calling. Admittedly, in practice, it might be hard to tell the two behaviour-patterns apart. But the scope of an ethic of investment is wider than this suggests – it would refer to all investible resources, not only those resulting from business profits.

The derivability of a 'Protestant investment ethic' from basic concepts of religious morality seems clear and undeniable. But was it actually derived? So far as explicit statements are concerned, the answer is, I think, 'almost'. We can see this from a consideration of two terms which crop up continually in the Puritan and Calvinist writers on economic activity, namely, 'gifts' and 'talents'. In modern English, the two terms are synonymous; both refer to useful or desirable abilities with which a person may be blessed (it is quite difficult even today to avoid terminology with religious connotations). They have the same meaning in the works of the Puritan/ Calvinist preachers of the sixteenth and seventeenth centuries, but the religious connotation of the terms is naturally much more self-conscious. The term 'talent' is of course Biblical in origin, and gives its name to a well-known parable, while 'gift' is understood to mean a gift of God – not, however, a free gift, but a gift entrusted to man (or some man, or woman) to be used in accordance with God's will. Since gifts and talents refer to human abilities, it was natural, and very common, for the Puritan and Calvinist writers to speak of them in connection with the particular calling. William Perkins, for example, in his *Treatise of the Callings or Vocations of Men*, enjoined Christians, in choosing an earthly calling, to 'examine for and to what calling [their gifts] are fittest', since God has bestowed gifts on us 'that they might be employed in his service' (Perkins 1970, pp. 459, 450). Richard Greenham agreed: God indicates to us the task we are called to do, that is, the right calling for us, by giving us the appropriate gifts; hence every man should 'search his own heart whereunto in affection and action he is most serviceable to God, and profitable to his brethren', and 'pursue specially this gift most carefully and continually' (Greenham 1605, p. 294). According to John Preston,

'Every excellency is a talent', and 'every man hath some talents' and 'must use them to his master's [that is, God's] advantage [and thereby] do good to men' by diligence in his calling (Preston 1636, p. 94). The Scottish divine William Struther likewise urged men, in their calling, to be 'diligent in the use of their talent', and explicitly equated talents and gifts: 'Our gift ... is our Talent' (Struther 1628, Cent. 1, p. 23).

Gifts and talents, then, are God-given abilities to be used in our earthly callings; but the terms have a further reference, namely, to material wealth, and thereby are linked also with the idea of stewardship. As the leading English Puritan William Ames quite typically puts it, riches, 'being designed for good use, are rightly called the gifts ... of god'; hence 'We must strive [by] all diligence to make riches our instrument of piety' (Ames 1639, Fourth Book, p. 253). Richard Baxter, explaining economic inequality, informed his readers that 'God giveth not to all alike: He putteth ten talents into the hands of one servant, and but one into another's'. However, *richesse oblige*: the more is given to a man, the more is required of him (Baxter 1673, p. 257). For Archbishop Ussher, as we have already seen, 'we are not absolute owners of the things we possess: but God's stewards who are enjoined to employ his talents to such uses as he requireth'.

The following conclusions can be inferred from our discussion of gifts and talents so far. Gifts and talents, in the sense of human abilities, should in the explicit opinion of the spokesmen of ascetic Protestantism, be devoted to men's earthly callings. Gifts and talents, in the sense of wealth or material resources, should in their opinion be devoted to works pleasing to God. Does this imply that gifts and talents, in the *latter* sense, should be devoted, *inter alia*, to aiding men's performance of their callings? In other words, do the spokesmen enunciate an explicit 'ethic of investment'? It is difficult to give a definite answer, not least because of the ambiguity, or wide application, of the vocabulary of gifts and talents. When those two terms are used, especially when their devotion to men's earthly callings is enjoined, it is often unclear whether human abilities, or material assets, or both, are intended. What exactly did Calvin mean when he wrote in his commentary on Psalm 127 that 'we should apply to use all the talents and advantages which [God] has conferred upon us' (Calvin 1843, p. 104); and in his commentary on the Parable of the Talents, that 'Those who use to advantage what God has deposited with them are said to trade ... and the industry with which each man prosecutes the task laid on him, and his very vocation ... and the rest of the gifts are reckoned as merchandise'(Calvin 1972, p. 288)? Only that these talents and gifts are *like* tradable assets, or that they *include* them? When the Scot David Dickson wrote, rather like Richard Baxter (see above), that 'As the master in the parable giveth not the same number of talents to each servant; so the Lord giveth not a like measure of gifts to everyone, but to some more, to some less' (Dickson 1651, p. 294), was he, like Baxter, referring to the unequal distribution of economic assets? If so, when he went on to say that 'As in the parable some made use of their talents, some not: so ... some employ the gifts they have, according to their calling, to the edifying of others and promoving of the kingdom of Christ, othersome make no conscience to promove Christ's kingdom in their vocation, as their duty set down in his Word doth require', he was in effect enjoining godly use of material assets in one's calling. But one cannot be sure that this is his meaning: it is equally possible that his words are a call to use one's natural abilities honestly and altruistically rather than selfishly. Again: when Baxter himself wrote, in justification of the pursuit of wealth in one's calling, that 'You are bound to improve all your Master's talents', in order that 'you may be the better provided to do God's service, and may do the more good with what you have' (Baxter 1673, p. 450), did he intend to include material assets among the 'talents' to be devoted to the acquisition of wealth? Again it is impossible to be sure. But at any rate one can perhaps say that, given the indubitably broad range of reference of the terms 'gifts' and 'talents', injunctions to 'improve' them could plausibly enough be taken as sanctioning investment of one's material assets in the work of one's calling. One cannot tell whether or to what extent Protestant businessmen thus interpreted the teachings of the divines.

However, a little more *can* be said about the subject. Some enlightenment may be gained by switching our attention for a moment from the divines to an eminent contemporary philosopher, John Locke (also, of course, a leading theorist and apologist of Protestant Christianity). In the opinion of a number of scholars, Locke's moral and social thought is founded on Puritan premises, including such 'Weberian' concepts as the calling and the work ethic.[1] Locke's famous justification of private property is of interest here, not so much for his founding it on labour, but rather for the link he postulates with productivity. Private property is justified, in Locke's eyes, because God gave the earth to men 'for their benefit and the greatest conveniences of life they were capable to draw from it'. According to Locke, a system of private property in land is the one best adapted to this end: 'he who appropriates land ... increases the common stock of mankind', Locke says (Locke 1966, p. 37). The clear implication is that landownership is justified by the productive use of the land by its owner; so a landowner, it would seem, has a duty to use his land productively. As Onora O'Neill has written on this point: 'The Parable of the Talents was never far from Locke's mind' (O'Neill 1981, p. 318).

If this reading of Locke is accepted, it suggests that, in the Puritan view, not only is there a duty to serve God and one's fellows by devoting one's time and abilities to one's earthly calling, but also (if Locke's view is representative) to use the natural resources one owns for the same purpose, by realizing their productive potential in an economic sense. From this it is only a small step to a general duty to use any non-human resources that one owns for the same end, in one's calling – in other words to an ethic of investment.

This step was, in fact, consciously taken in one case at least, by the Scottish divine John Cockburn, as appears from the following passage in his book, *Jacob's Vow*:

> If one keeps the wealth by him which he stands not in need of, if he hoard it up in his chest and coffers, and put it to no use, what is he the better of it? ... Dionysius the Elder, understanding a certain citizen had gold in his house, he commanded it to be brought to him; but afterwards when the same person went to sojourn in another city, and did trade with a little which he had stolen away; Dionysius sent for him, and restored him all back again, because he began to use his wealth, and to leave off rendering an useful thing useless; thereby showing that the true use of money is not to hoard it up, but to lay it out in such and such ways as tend to the public good (Cockburn 1686, p. 79).

Cockburn here gives a clear religious sanction for investing one's money in a useful calling. One swallow does not make a summer, and one quotation does not make an ethic. Still, I have suggested that other birds we have noticed may be swallows too, though less clearly so than in Cockburn's case.

Inner-worldly asceticism and business success

An ethic of investment prescribes a certain relationship between means and ends; but it also implies something else that is relevant to the Weber Thesis, namely, what may be called a long-term perspective. The essence of investment – for whatever purpose, be it the public good or private profit – is that the benefits that could be derived now from certain resources are postponed, for the sake of a greater future benefit. Investment, therefore, implies self-restraint or, in other words, a kind of asceticism. The ethic of investment I have been postulating thus illustrates the two-sided nature of Weber's Protestant ethic in general, that is, its combination of asceticism and service to the public good. By asceticism, I mean self-denial seen as good in itself (puritanism, in the everyday sense of the word); but self-denial can also be for the sake and benefit of others. Both these themes are combined, perhaps even conflated, in the writings of the divines we have been studying. There is thus a certain parallel between the 'primary Protestant ethic' and the way of life of the paradigmatic capitalist businessman who, in the search for greater long-term profits, foregoes possible gratification in the short term (a phenomenon referred to by some economists as 'abstinence'). This, to repeat, is a parallelism, not a logical connection between the Protestant ethic and the spirit of capitalism; but it has its significance, as we shall see.

For one thing, it suggests a likely *psychological* similarity between adepts of the two life-styles, ascetic Protestant and profit-maximizing businessman, such that the former could serve as a facilitator for the latter, despite the differences of aims. But secondly, the parallel between the godly and the economically successful life was noticed, and frequently invoked, by the Puritan preachers themselves. One example is James Janeway:

> Believe it, sirs, heaven and glory are not got with sitting still with our hands in our pockets. We think it worth the while to rise early, and to sit up late, to get an earthly estate ... The poor countryman ploughs and sows, harrows, reaps [etc., etc.] before he can eat his bread; shall we look for a rich crop, and do nothing at all but eat, drink and sleep? Is this the way to be rich? Is this the way to be happy for ever? If you intend to do anything in religion to any purpose, you must buckle to your business ... You must take as much pains about your souls as men do about their bodies or estates (Janeway 1847, p. 275).

The same idea – of a parallel between worldly and heavenly rewards, or rather the ways of life that lead to them – was put into doggerel verse by the well-known Puritan divine (and commentator on the Westminster Shorter Catechism)[2] John Flavell:

> None will deny, but those are blessed pains
> Which are attended with the richest gains
> Grant this, and then most clearly tis inferred
> Soul-work to all deserves to be preferred.
> This is an unknown Trade. Oh, who can count
> To what the gains of godliness amount? (Flavell 1701, p. 16).

Besides this parallel or analogy of life-styles, there is also, of course, an obvious causal connection between the godly life ('ascetic Protestantism') and business success. The significance of this is not quite what is usually thought. It does not vindicate the Weber Thesis; rather the parallel and the causal connection together seen to have led, in the minds of a number of writers, to a remarkable conflation, and even confusion, of the two spheres. Quite often, when clerical propagandists refer to the 'gain' or 'profit' to be derived from godly behaviour, it is difficult to know whether worldly or spiritual advantages are meant. It cannot be excluded that the equivocation was deliberate. Here, at any rate, are some examples. James Janeway, who was quoted above, also gave the following instructions to 'masters' in his *Duties of Masters and Servants*:

> Take heed of idleness, carelessness, and trusting your servants too much. A master's negligence tempts the servant to unfaithfulness. When masters are idle abroad, usually the servants are so at home. It can't well be expected, that when the master is spending his time foolishly and unaccountably in the coffee-houses, ale-houses or taverns, the servant should spend his wisely in the shop; especially when he observes that the master never ... examines his books, nor calls him to any account. O this sin of idleness, that sodomitical, soul-debasing [and] estate-wasting sin! Sir, do you never take a Bible in your hands? Do you never read how much God is displeased with sloth; how oft he forbids it? (Janeway 1676, p. 448)

The reader of this passage is likely to be a little bewildered at the way what seems at first to be simply utilitarian advice about sensible business practice switches to denunciation of sin and invocation of the will of God. Does Janeway, one might wonder, detest idleness and carelessness more on account of their 'soul-debasing' or their 'estate-wasting' nature? Does he confuse godliness and sound business conduct, or is his message rather that idleness is contrary to both? Perhaps he cannot quite be convicted of confusion. With other clerical writers, however, the confusion is beyond question. An example is Richard Steele, author of *The Tradesman's Calling*, who figures prominently as a target of R.H. Tawney in his classic *Religion and the Rise of Capitalism*. Steele was keenly aware of the material benefits of godliness, and given to quoting the Biblical tag, 'The hand of the diligent maketh rich'. Having noted that diligence is a Christian virtue, and that the Christian therefore makes it his 'care and business to serve God in his calling', he continues thus:

> The tradesman's diligence consists, in laying hold of opportunities. For if a man be never so industrious and painful, yet unless he be watchful to observe

his opportunity, and then swift to lay hold thereon, he is wanting in the diligence requisite for him ... Opportunities, if caught by the forelock, will pay for all the care and watching for them (Steele 1684, p. 77).

What kind of opportunities, one might ask? Opportunities to serve God in one's calling, or opportunities to make a profit? It seems fairly clear that Steele is referring to the latter, but he never explains why this is a religious duty, except for suggesting (implausibly) that it is a necessary part of the Christian virtue of diligence. But he is quick to add a religious analogy:

Thus the Kingdom of Heaven is compared ... to a Merchant-Man seeking goodly pearls: who when he had found one pearl of great price, he went and sold all he had, and bought that pearl. He spied his opportunity, and struck in with it to his great advantage; and so must the diligent tradesman do (Steele 1684, p. 81).

Steele's moral here is certainly *not* that the tradesman should sell his stock and devote himself to religion; rather, Steele is praising business acumen by conflating it with religion.

Steele is by no means the only example of such conflation. Another, even more blatant example is provided by James Clark, a Glasgow merchant-turned-minister who may be called the Scottish Richard Steele. Clark is the author of a remarkable tract with a remarkable title: *The Spiritual-Merchant: or, the Art of Merchandizing Spiritualized. Directing how to be rich towards God, and also how to acquire worldly wealth.* Clark's title may seem unusually crass, but it really expresses in open and unguarded form the message of Steele's book also. Like Steele, and many another ascetic Protestant spokesman, he quotes the favourite passage from Proverbs, 'the hand of the diligent maketh rich' (Clark 1701, p. 126; Steele 1684, p. 92). He also uses the concepts of 'talents' and 'stewardship', in such a way as to suggest that to increase one's wealth is a religious duty, but without giving any explanation why: 'Ye shall shortly be called to an account of your stewardship, how ye have husbanded and managed your affairs: how ye have spent your time, how ye have improven your talents' (Clark 1701, p. 130). Clark might here be taken to be expressing what I have called the ethic of investment, but it is more likely that he wishes to conflate godliness and good business. This is suggested by the following remarkable but not uncharacteristic juxtaposition of ideas:

O Christian Merchants ... that ye may daily increase your spiritual stock, that ye may be waxing rich towards God, and laying up treasures in Heaven ... these rules and directions may be considered ...

1.   Endeavour to have a true sense of your want and need ... Be earnest in prayer to God for a discovery of the true state of your souls, how naked, how poor, how wretched you are ...

3.   Ye must be skilful in arithmetic and merchant-account book-keeping, this is so very needful that a man cannot be a complete merchant or manage trade to any good effect without it (Clark 1701, p. 133).

Clark then proceeds into a detailed discussion of the advantages of Italian book-keeping methods, apparently oblivious of his transition from treasures in Heaven to treasures on earth. It is instructive, too, that Clark can press into service the edifying verse of 'Mr Flavel', of which an extract was given above (p. 91), and which Clark cites with evident approval (Clark 1701, p. 159). Flavell, as we saw, wished to draw an *analogy* between 'the gains of godliness' and the material rewards of trade. But in Clark's hands, the analogy has become almost an identity. Whereas for Flavell the expression 'gains of godliness' refers to spiritual benefits, for Clark it has precisely the ambiguity he desires, and refers to spiritual and material rewards equally.

Steele and Clark are no doubt extreme cases, at least in their naïvety (though in fairness it should be added that both continually stress the necessity of honest dealing), so that one might be tempted to dismiss them as marginal, unrepresentative figures. However, this would be a mistake, because what clearly leads to their conflation of religion and business is just the fact that the very same behaviour (what I call Weber's primary Protestant ethic) is prescribed by both. The significance of this is much wider. What it leads to is not a profit ethic, so much as a kind of collusion between religion and business, or between ascetic Protestantism and nascent capitalism (Weber himself might have called it an 'elective affinity'). The spokesmen of ascetic Protestantism could point out to businessmen that virtue is profitable, as an inducement to virtue; businessmen, receptive to the message, could have two reasons (I shall not speculate as to which weighed more with them) for favouring virtue and religion. All of this, of course, depends on the assumption that businessmen in any case seek profits, regardless of any religious doctrines. James Clark, in fact, said so explicitly: 'Every man by trading purposes profit, and desires to be prosperous, the which ends are achieved most surely and most speedily by being industrious in our lawful affairs' (Clark 1701, p. 126). Clark's words reveal an untroubled acceptance of the profit-motive, but no *injunction* to maximize profit, such as is found in Weber's Protestant profit ethic.

Clark's *Spiritual-Merchant* reprints sermons delivered in 1689. A few years later, as the seventeenth century drew to a close, what I have called the collusion of religion and business is revealed again in a famous or notorious Scottish enterprise, the ill-fated project to found a trading colony in Darien. The collusion also points to an interesting ambiguity in the Biblical tag, 'the hand of the diligent maketh rich'. Whose hand makes whom rich? In a capitalist situation, profit accrues to the entrepreneur not only from his own diligence, but also from that of his workers. Thus we find William Paterson, the Scottish founder of the Bank of England who was also the moving spirit behind the Darien scheme, expressing himself in a letter to his collaborator in the latter enterprise, Principal Dunlop of Glasgow University, as 'very anxious to have a good magistracy so much as possible for a good beginning and foundation of a Ministry which will be of the highest consequence to this design'.[3] To the Rev. Alexander Shields, assigned to the Expedition (along with three other ministers) by the Church of Scotland, Paterson wrote: 'Above all things, endeavour to cultivate the reverence and respect for God and his religion; for in this there is great gain, not only in eternity, but even in time ...'[4] That the Kirk itself agreed is shown by a letter to the Darien colonists from the Commission of the General Assembly:

> Are you not convinced that sobriety, temperance, diligence and all other moral and Christian virtues are truly your temporal, as well as your eternal interest; and that your worldly affairs cannot thrive without these ... ? Your temporal as well as your spiritual and eternal gain shall be great, if you improve your talent, and manage the price put into your hands, wisely and well ... Patient diligence and industry will overcome your first difficulties, and through the blessing of God, you shall find the promise made out to you, *That the hand of the diligent maketh rich.*[5]

In view of the subsequent history, these words make rather poignant reading. In the event, the colony went down to total disaster, an outcome which both the ministers, and the Directors of the Expedition in Edinburgh, were inclined to blame on the hopelessly ungodly behaviour of the colonists. As the Directors put it, after alluding in an Address to the vicious and intemperate lives led by their men in Darien: 'Nor can we, upon serious reflection, wonder if an enterprise of this nature has misgiven in the hands of such as ... neither feared God nor regarded man'.[6]

Benjamin Franklin, Daniel Defoe, and Adam Smith

Before moving on to the next stage of the argument, it is time once again to take stock. What has been established so far is that what I have called a Protestant profit ethic did exist in seventeenth century Britain, though it was one whose logical relation to capitalistic profit-seeking is somewhat problematic. There also existed what I have called a collusion between ascetic Protestantism and capitalistic business, based on the coincidence of Protestant and business virtues. Weber, however, found his paradigmatic example of the 'spirit of capitalism' in eighteenth century America, in the writings of Benjamin Franklin. According to Weber, these writings express a 'capitalist profit ethic', the nature of which was set out in some detail in the first chapter of this book. I shall argue that Weber was mistaken. What is expressed in Franklin's work is not a profit ethic, but another recognition of the coincidence of Protestant and business virtues – or in other words, of the happy fact that religious virtue is profitable.

That Franklin was a child of New England Puritanism there can be no doubt whatever. Born in Boston, he tells us in his *Autobiography* that he was 'educated as a Presbyterian'; though he also tells us, significantly, that he found the dogmas of that faith, 'such as "eternal decrees of God", "election", "reprobation" etc.', unacceptable and even unintelligible. On the other hand, the moral training of his upbringing left their mark on his character. Franklin's father, he tells us, 'frequently repeated' to him a passage from the Book of Proverbs which was a favourite with the Puritan preachers: 'Seest thou a man diligent in his calling, he shall stand before kings, he shall not stand before mean men' (Franklin 1924, pp. 106-7). Somewhat later, he 'conceived a bold and arduous project of arriving at moral perfection', defined by 'thirteen names of virtues', including temperance, order, frugality and industry (Franklin 1924, pp. 109-10). But in what light, exactly, did Franklin view these virtues? Industry, he tells us, he had early seen 'as a means of obtaining wealth and distinction'. As for his regime of moral perfection, he comments that 'to this little artifice, with the blessing of God', he 'owed the constant felicity of his life ... To Temperance he ascribes his long-continued health ... , to Industry and Frugality, the early easiness of his circumstances and acquisition of his fortune'. There is, Franklin concludes, 'Nothing so likely to make a man's fortune as virtue' (Franklin 1924, pp. 119-20). This, he makes clear, is the lesson he wishes to inculcate.

And so he did, in his famous pedagogic tracts, from two of which Weber quotes in his essay: namely, *Advice to a Young Tradesman*, and *Necessary Hints to Those That Would be Rich* (Weber 1930, p. 192). The very title of the latter indicates Franklin's view clearly enough: pursuit of wealth is *not* obligatory in a moral or any other sense, though Franklin clearly assumes that it is a widespread motive. The 'necessary hints', therefore, are, in Kantian terms, only hypothetical, not categorical imperatives. The same point is made explicit in *Advice to a Young Tradesman*, in a passage not cited by Weber: 'The way to wealth, *if you desire it*, is as plain as the way to market. It depends chiefly on two words, *industry* and *frugality*; that is, waste neither *time* nor *money*, but make the best use of both' (Franklin 1882, Vol. II, p. 87). I have emphasized the words, 'if you desire it', in this passage, because they make it plain that, morally speaking, pursuit of wealth is not obligatory. But Franklin naturally assumed that tradesmen are in business for the sake of profit; as he put it in his *Principles of Trade*, 'The spring or movement of [commerce] is, and ever must be, gain or the hopes of gain ... Gain is the first mover ... of all intercourse and trade' (Franklin 1882, Vol. II, p. 385).[7]

Perhaps the best account of Franklin's views on the subject is his piece entitled *The Way to Wealth*, published under the pseudonym Richard Saunders, as 'Poor Richard's Almanac for the year of our Lord 1758'. This brief *summa* of Franklin's philosophy is so pertinent and perfect in its way as almost to merit reproduction in full, but I will content myself with a few extracts. Franklin in this essay constructs a little drama, in which his *alter ego*, Father Abraham, addresses a group of merchants who have been grumbling about the 'badness of the times', especially the 'heavy taxes' that are in their view ruining the country. Abraham admonishes them thus:

Friends ... We are taxed twice as much by our Idleness, three times as much by our Pride, and four times as much by our Folly ... Let us hearken to good advice ... *God helps them that help themselves*, as *Poor Richard* says ...

If Time be of all things the most precious, *wasting Time*, must be, as *Poor Richard* says, the greatest prodigality ...

He that hath a Trade hath an Estate, and He that hath a Calling hath an Office of Profit and Honour; but then the *Trade* must be worked at, and the *Calling* well followed ... *God gives all things to Industry* ...

Methinks I hear some of you say, *Must a Man afford himself no Leisure*? ... *Poor Richard* says, *Employ thy Time well if thou meanest to gain Leisure* ... Industry gives Comfort and Plenty ... *Fly Pleasures, and they'll follow you* ...

So much for Industry, my friends ... but we must add *Frugality*, if we would make our *Industry* more certainly successful ... *If you would be wealthy, ... think of Saving as well as Getting ...*

Get what you can, and what you get hold;
Tis the Stone that will turn all your Lead into Gold (Franklin 1924, pp. 237-40, 244).

The message is clear enough. The end is prosperity; industry and frugality are means only. Father Abraham (or Poor Richard, or Benjamin Franklin) is offering good advice, not preaching a moral code. To be sure, the means to success are seen as virtues, but only in the sense that they involve deliberate and perhaps painful self-constraint for the sake of long-run advantage. Or perhaps not only in this sense, since it is obvious that the virtuous means have a religious ancestry, and derive from the primary Protestant ethic. Nevertheless, for Franklin, earning more and more money is not an end in itself, still less a moral *summum bonum*: the ends are comfort, plenty, leisure, and pleasures. Gratification is indeed to be postponed, but not indefinitely – certainly not beyond the grave. So far as an ethical aura still clings to Franklin's worldly advice, it clings to the means, not the end. I do not deny that Franklin's philosophy constitutes a spirit of capitalism, well calculated to promote economic development, nor do I deny its ascetic Protestant roots: what I deny, against Weber, is that it expresses a profit ethic.

My interpretation of Franklin can be strengthened by turning to another dispenser of advice to tradesmen, who wrote earlier and much more voluminously than Franklin did, but in a very similar vein – the English nonconformist Daniel Defoe. The business of the tradesman, says Defoe bluntly, is to get money; that is 'what he opens his shop for or keeps his warehouse for' (Defoe 1727, pp. 35-6). Defoe refers frequently to the tradesman's 'calling'; but while he is consistently deferential to religion and piety, it never occurs to him to interpret this 'calling' in religious terms. On the contrary, he explicitly distinguishes 'business and calling' from 'duties of religion' – the latter have to do with a future life, the former with the present life (Defoe 1726, p. 61). In brief, Defoe's attitude to business, writing in 1726, is completely secular, despite the high importance he attaches to religion. Yet, as with Franklin, his advice to tradesmen is replete with echoes of the Puritan ethic. Diligence is recommended and sloth deplored, by citing the familiar passages from the Book of Proverbs. The good use of God-given time is enjoined, while lengthy warnings are given against 'immoderate expense' and 'immoderate pleasure'.

The right use of money for tradesmen is to invest it: they must 'frugally lay up their gain, in order to increase their gain' (Defoe 1726, pp. 53, 61, 118f., 134, 319). The way of life recommended is said by Defoe to be the businessman's duty – not, however, for religious reasons, but because his calling requires it. This is a point of some importance – Defoe is explicit that his prescriptions apply only to tradesmen, not to all men: 'Pleasures and diversions may be innocent in themselves, which are not so to him [the tradesman]'. Like Franklin, Defoe prescribes honesty as a means to credit which 'is the tradesman's life' (Defoe 1726, pp. 119, 235). What we have here is clearly not a universal Puritan ethic, but a code of prudent business practice.

This means that there is a difference, of some significance, between Defoe and Franklin, which may make Defoe seem closer than Franklin to Weber's spirit of capitalism. Whereas Franklin enunciates a philosophy of life, Defoe confines himself to an account of the tradesman's role or calling. For this reason, pursuit of money profit bulks larger for Defoe than for Franklin (though it bulks large for both). Not only does Defoe state what he takes to be obvious, that the point of trade is to get money, he prescribes, in accordance with Weber's spirit of capitalism, that the tradesman must seek *maximum* profit. The tradesman's business, he says is 'getting money by *all* possible [fair] methods' (Defoe 1727, p. 167, emphasis added). He speaks, with obvious approval, of the tradesman 'always looking sharp out, watching advantages and then taking hold of them, improving every hint, pushing every visible advantage', a description reminiscent of the Rev. Richard Steele's version of the good tradesman fifty years earlier: 'watchful to observe his opportunity, and then swift to lay hold thereon' (see above, p. 93), as well as of other Puritan writers who dwelt on the duty to 'improve the opportunities' of one's calling.[8] In other words, Defoe's advice, just as rooted in ascetic Protestantism as Franklin's, seems aimed only at the goal of 'earning more and more money', for (unlike in Franklin's case) no other is mentioned. This however could well be misleading, just because Defoe is concerned only with the professional duties of the businessman, not with life as a whole. It is therefore quite compatible with Defoe's prescriptions that he saw the money to be accumulated by following them, as a means to similar ends as those envisaged by Franklin. In any case, the acquisition of money is not seen by Defoe as a moral duty, even although the means to it are (thanks at least in part to the Protestant inheritance) seen as virtues.

No quotations from the Book of Proverbs, or any other part of Holy

Writ, are to be found in either of the two masterpieces of Adam Smith, *The Theory of Moral Sentiments* and *The Wealth of Nations*, despite the fact that their author was a Scotsman brought up and educated in one of the world's most Calvinist societies. However, considerable attention is given in both works to honesty, industry and frugality, those virtues that bulk so large in the thinking of Franklin and Defoe. Smith also, in the *Theory of Moral Sentiments*, treats them as virtues, to be precise, virtues characteristic of the 'middling and inferior' ranks of people, rather than those in 'the superior states of life'. The reason is, says Smith, that for the former, but not the latter, virtue and self-interest coincide: 'the road to virtue, and that to fortune ... are, happily, in most cases, very nearly the same'; fortunately, this applies to 'by far the greater part of mankind' (Smith 1976, p. 63). Thus Smith in the character of, so to speak, sociologist of morals. But as moral philosopher he tells a somewhat different tale, and one that ties virtue and self-interest even more tightly together. As moral philosopher, Smith offers a general theory to explain what it is that constitutes virtue – what makes virtue virtue, that is – and his well-known answer is that virtue is that which is approved by the sympathetic impartial spectator, the spectator who sympathizes impartially with the feelings of all affected by a given kind of behaviour (all moral persons have internalized this impartial spectator). It follows that one major department of virtue is the virtues of prudence, those forms of behaviour that promote the happiness of the agent. So long as no one else is harmed by such actions, the impartial spectator must approve of them, and therefore they are virtues. Industry and frugality are such virtues (at least for the greater part of mankind). But they are also virtues of 'self-command', or deferred gratification: they involve 'steadily sacrificing the ease and enjoyment of the present moment for the probable expectation of the still greater ease and enjoyment of a more distant but more lasting period of time' (Smith 1976, p. 215).

Smith's moral theory is not wholly secular. In his view, moral laws are laws of God, and the internalized impartial spectator that approves virtuous and condemns vicious actions is the 'vicegerent' of God within us. Smith's theology, however, is very un-Calvinist: man's moral faculty approves that which furthers the happiness of mankind, because 'the happiness of mankind ... seems to have been the original purpose intended by the Author of nature, when he brought them into existence' (Smith 1976, p. 166). And yet this un-Calvinist view converges with that expressed by many spokesmen of ascetic Protestantism. Thanks to God's scheme of beneficence, in Smith's view, in this world 'every virtue naturally meets with its proper reward, with the recompense which is most fit to encourage and promote it'. And 'What is the reward most proper for encouraging industry, prudence and circumspection? Success in every sort of business ... Wealth and external honours are their proper recompense, and the recompense which they can seldom fail of acquiring'. Smith's morality includes a profit ethic, in that what is profitable is *ipso facto* virtuous (other things equal); and this is because moral virtue and self-interest are not separate, but overlap.

Thus according to Smith's moral psychology, as expounded in *The Theory of Moral Sentiments*, two motives induce in us a propensity to the economic virtues of industry and frugality – our self-interest and our moral sense – and in both regards this is ultimately due to the beneficent dispositions of the Deity. In *The Wealth of Nations*, there occur both a change of emphasis (naturally enough) and a significant modification. Industry and frugality are still treated as virtues, but the moral motivation to behave in these ways drops out of sight, while the motive of self-interest is, notoriously, emphasized. But there is also a modification. Smith revises his view that self-interest prompts to these virtues 'by far the greater part of mankind'. His perspective on this now becomes more historical and sociological. Since industry and frugality are virtues of self-command, requiring the sacrificing of present for future benefit, they depend on the existence of these future benefits, in other words on an appropriate socio-economic structure, offering appropriate incentives. So far as industry is concerned, 'The wages of labour are the encouragement of industry, which, like every other human quality, improves in proportion to the encouragement it receives' (Smith 1961, Vol. I, p. 91). Smith mentions two historical factors bearing on this, 'the fall of the feudal system, and ... the establishment of a government which afforded to industry the only encouragement which it requires, some tolerable security that it shall enjoy the fruits of its own labour' (Smith 1961, Vol. I, p. 264). As to feudalism, Smith explains that, 'in every country, the general character of the inhabitants as to industry or idleness' depends on the funds used respectively to 'support' the two opposed lifestyles:

> We are more industrious than our forefathers; because in the present times the funds destined for the maintenance of industry are much greater in proportion to those which are likely to be employed in the maintenance of idleness, than they were two or three centuries ago. Our ancestors were idle for want of a sufficient encouragement to industry. It is better, says the proverb, to play for nothing than to work for nothing (Smith 1961, Vol. I, p. 356).

In other words, says Smith, 'Wherever capital predominates, industry prevails' over idleness (Smith 1961, Vol. I, p. 358). Capitalism, then, but not feudalism, provides incentives to industry, and makes industry advantageous. This means, according to the philosophy of *The Theory of Moral Sentiments* that (though Smith does not say so), capitalism, or as Smith would call it, commercial society, has made industry much more of a virtue than ever before in human history.

The virtue of frugality is treated rather differently by Smith in *The Wealth of Nations*. In the first place, frugality is the virtue that creates capital, while the opposing vice, prodigality, destroys it (Smith 1961, Vol. I, pp. 358-62). But does not frugality require incentives also: does it not 'like every other human quality, improve in proportion to the encouragement it receives'? Smith seems to think such encouragement unnecessary, because of the power, in almost all men, of 'the desire of bettering our condition, a desire which, though generally calm and dispassionate, comes with us from the womb, and never leaves us till we go into the grave'. This, says Smith, prompts us to save. Hence 'in the greater part of men ... , the principle of frugality seems not only to predominate, but to predominate very greatly' (Smith 1961, Vol. I, pp. 362-3). This assessment, however, is not consistent with what Smith says about feudalism, which he describes as a regime of lavish expenditure, on maintaining 'a multitude of retainers and dependants', on warfare, and on extravagant hospitality, just because no markets existed on which the products of landed property could be traded (Smith 1961, Vol. I, p. 433). All in all, therefore, Smith's view must be taken to be (even if he does not explicitly say so), that frugality too is pre-eminently a virtue of commercial society, or of capitalism.

As for the rise of capitalism itself (or the downfall of feudalism), Smith attributes this purely to political factors and to the effects of commerce itself, which he sees as an expression of human nature (the famous 'propensity of mankind to truck and barter'). No role, or only an extremely minor role, is ascribed to religion, and none whatever to Protestantism as such. Puritanism is explained by Smith as an effect, not suggested as a cause. As we know, Smith held that in class-divided societies, the middling and inferior ranks of the people (but not the superior ranks) esteem industry, frugality and honesty as prime virtues. As he puts it in *The Wealth of Nations*, the common people adhere to a strict and austere morality, the higher orders to a 'liberal, or, if you will [a] loose' one. According to Smith, almost all religious sects begin among the common people, and therefore adopt the austere system of morality (Smith 1961, Vol. II, pp. 315-6). However,

Smith notes that urbanization, because of the anonymity of city life, threatens the effectiveness of moral pressures – and here religion, or rather the small religious sect, can provide a solution, by subjecting the deracinated city-dweller, once again, to moral oversight or supervision (Smith 1961, Vol. II, p. 317). This is as close as Smith comes to any agreement with Weber. To the doctrinal differences between different creeds Smith attributes no causal significance whatever.

Should we say that this view, on the part of the founder of the economic theory of capitalism, discredits Weber, or should we rather say that it betrays a remarkable blindness on the part of Smith? In view of all the evidence reviewed in this book, to say nothing of Froude's judgment of the Scottish character in 1865, I am inclined to say the latter. Nevertheless, as we have seen, Smith did not leave theology out of his system. It is thanks to God's beneficence towards men that 'every virtue naturally meets with its proper reward', and is thereby encouraged. In *The Wealth of Nations*, however, this is qualified: Smith's disparaging remarks about feudalism make clear that the divine harmony of virtue and reward hardly operates in that system. Rather, it is the capitalist free market system that best realizes God's beneficent plan. In that system, an economic agent who 'intends only his own gain [is] led by an invisible hand to promote an end which was no part of his intention' – the general interest. The impartial spectator of *The Theory of Moral Sentiments*, duly enlightened by the economic theory expounded in *The Wealth of Nations*, would unhesitatingly give his approbation. In capitalist commercial society, virtue and self-interest coincide as never before. They coincide to such a degree, that moral motives can be to a significant degree dispensed with (not entirely, of course), and self-interest safely relied on. Smith, in this way, has created an economic theory of capitalism posited largely on the pursuit of self-interest, and correspondingly little on moral obligation. This is a 'spirit of capitalism' quite different from Weber's.

It did not, however, completely displace a more Weberian one. Ever since Smith wrote, defenders of capitalism have been able to avail themselves, and have availed themselves, of two distinct lines of argument. One, derived from Smith, freely concedes that capitalism is based on and rewards the pursuit of self-interest (Smith himself was no admirer of capital*ists*, as distinct from capital*ism*) but justifies it by the capacity of the free market to turn self-interest to the public good (Friedrich Hayek has been the subtlest and most distinguished exemplar of this theory in the present century). The other, more

Weberian, defends capitalism on the grounds that it rewards, and thereby elicits, moral virtues such as industry and frugality which seem to be secularized descendants of the Protestant ethic. Neither, however, invokes a profit ethic in a strictly Weberian sense. Nineteenth century Britain often seemed to prefer the quasi-Weberian justification, as witness the huge popularity of the writings of Samuel Smiles (celebrator, in four volumes, of the virtues of *Thrift, Self-Help, Character* and *Duty*); or this passage in Andrew Ure's celebrated *Philosophy of Manufactures* (published in 1835):

> The mill-owner who has a nice sense of purity in heart and life, and just comprehension of his own interests, and a conscientious concern for the well-being of his dependants, will adopt every practicable measure to raise the standard of their behaviour ... It is excessively the interest of every mill-owner to organize his moral machinery on equally sound principles with his mechanical, for otherwise he will never command the steady hands, watchful eyes, and prompt cooperation, essential to excellence of product. Improvident work-people are apt to be reckless, and dissolute ones to be diseased: thus both are ill-qualified to discharge the delicate labour of automatic industry ... There is, in fact, no case in which the Gospel truth "Godliness is great gain" is more applicable than to the administration of an extensive factory ... It is therefore, as much for the advantage as it is the duty of every factory proprietor, to observe, in reference to his operatives, the divine injunction of loving his neighbours as himself (Ure 1835, pp. 416-8).

It is perhaps not entirely irrelevant that both Smiles and Ure were born and brought up in Scotland.

7 Postscript on the modern world

> The Puritan wanted to work in a calling; we are forced to do so; for when asceticism was carried out of monastic cells into everyday life, and began to dominate worldly morality, it did its part in building the tremendous cosmos of the modern economic order. This order is now bound to the technical and economic conditions of machine production which to-day determine the lives of all the individuals who are born into this mechanism, not only those directly concerned with economic acquisition, with irresistible force ... In Baxter's view the care for external goods should only lie on the shoulders of the saint 'like a light cloak, which can be thrown aside at any moment'. But fate decreed that the cloak should become an iron cage.
>
> Since asceticism undertook to remodel the world and to work out its ideas in the world, material goods have gained an increasing and finally an inexorable power over the lives of men as at no previous period in history. Today the spirit of religious asceticism – whether finally, who knows? – has escaped from the cage. But victorious capitalism, since it rests on mechanical foundations, needs its support no longer.

These words are quoted from the deservedly famous conclusion of Weber's great essay (Weber 1930, p. 181). They express, among other things, an acute awareness of the negative side of life in modern capitalist civilization. While Weber understood and fully accepted Adam Smith's argument as to the unmatched efficiency (or, as he himself put it elsewhere, economic rationality) of the capitalist market system, nevertheless it forces us to live in an 'iron cage' in which modern man is ruled by material goods with 'inexorable power'. Here Weber seems to echo Marx in the latter's antipathy to capitalist 'alienation' of human existence. However Weber was totally free of Marx's naive belief that capitalism could be straightforwardly replaced by an alternative system both more humane *and* more efficient, and so he could not hate capitalism with Marx's single-minded ferocity. Nor, unlike Marx, did he claim any ability to foretell the future course of human history. His analysis is of the past, and of the present. The present is capitalism, religious asceticism is of the past: it has given birth to capitalism, and died, or perhaps rather been killed by its offspring (together with the other elements of Western secular rationalism which also, in Weber's view, were in greater or lesser degree its progeny). Although Weber appears not to rule out entirely a rebirth of the historic religion, he can hardly have thought it likely, in view of his general theory of the history of modern Western civilization as inexorable 'disenchantment'.

Today, nearly a century after Weber wrote, nothing essential seems to have changed, except that the forces he portrayed appear stronger than ever. Capitalism now reigns supreme, and to an unprecedented degree, unchallenged; less than ever has it any need of support from the 'ascetic Protestantism' described by Weber, which seems, now, totally insignificant as a motivating force. Or does it?

We are told we must work, and use our talents to create wealth. "If a man will not work he shall not eat", wrote St Paul to the Thessalonians ... Nevertheless, the Tenth Commandment – Thou shalt not covet – recognises that money and owning things could become selfish activities. But it is not the creation of wealth that is wrong, but love of money for its own sake.

The spiritual dimension comes in deciding what one does with the wealth. How could we respond to the many calls for help, or invest in the future ... unless we had first worked hard and used our talents to create the necessary wealth? ...

None of this, of course, tells us exactly what kind of political and social institutions we should have ... What is certain, however, is that any set of social and economic arrangements which is not founded on the acceptance of individual responsibility will do nothing but harm ... You recall that Timothy was warned by St Paul that anyone who neglects to provide for his own house (meaning his family) has disowned the faith and is "worse than an infidel" ...

In our generation, the only way we can ensure that no-one is left without sustenance, help, or opportunity, is to have laws to provide for health and education, pensions for the elderly, succour for the sick and disabled. But intervention by the State must never become so great that it effectively removes personal responsibility. The same applies to taxation, for while you and I would work extremely hard whatever the circumstances, there are undoubtedly some who would not unless the incentive was there. And we need their efforts too.

These are the words of Margaret Thatcher, when Prime Minister of the United Kingdom, addressing – appropriately – the General Assembly of the Church of Scotland in Edinburgh in May, 1988 (the so-called 'Sermon on the Mound').[1] The echoes of the Weber Thesis are startling. Here is the work ethic, the injunction to use our 'talents' in pursuit of wealth, the justification of pursuing wealth in terms of its right use, above all in helping the needy (though not the idle and irresponsible).[2] These, it seems, are the convictions of a political leader who enjoyed Britain's longest premiership of this century, and consciously and deliberately set out to re-make her country's social and economic structure. To what extent she succeeded is a controversial issue, and at this point in history it is doubtless too early to reach anything like a definitive verdict. Nevertheless, her success, in the short run at least, has been, I believe, very considerable. As a result of the phenomenon known as 'Thatcherism', the intellectual and moral climate of Britain has become far more favourable than it was a couple of decades ago to 'wealth creation', 'enterprise', the 'free market' – in a word, to capitalism. At a practical level, capitalist wealth creation and enterprise have been encouraged by sharply reduced taxation on high incomes, by economic deregulation, and by the curbing of countervailing powers such as the trades unions; the scope of capitalism has been extended by privatization of nationalized industries; and the public services have been subjected, in various ways, to the ethos of capitalist business. In brief, Britain has become a much more undilutedly 'capitalist' society than at any time since the Second World War. This may mark a historical turning point. Nor has the historical significance of Thatcherism necessarily been confined to Britain. Similar trends, discernible in many other countries, may owe something to Thatcherism's pioneering example, and thereby to the unusually clear political vision of Margaret Thatcher who, as we have seen, explicitly connects her policies with ethical principles that bulk large in the Weber Thesis. Are these what Weber called the ghosts of dead religious beliefs prowling about in our secularized lives, or do they betoken the survival, or the rebirth, of the Protestant ethic in happy union with the spirit of capitalism?

Margaret Thatcher has often publicly described herself as a Christian, but not, so far as I know, as a Protestant (possibly too sectarian a label for a modern British politician to embrace). But however that may be, the fact is that she was brought up as a strict Methodist. Her father, Alderman Alfred Roberts, owner of a grocer's shop, was a popular Methodist lay preacher, and trustee of ten churches in Lincolnshire besides the Methodist Church in Finkin Street, Grantham, where Mr and Mrs Roberts regularly attended for many years. Mrs Roberts too was 'very religious', and church work 'played quite a large part' in the early life of their daughter Margaret. Margaret Thatcher 'had a very strict upbringing. We were never allowed to go to a cinema on Sunday', or to play cards or even snakes and ladders on that day. Mr Roberts was a strict Sabbatarian, who, in his capacity as local politician and later Alderman and Mayor, 'for years' opposed the opening of municipal parks, swimming pools and tennis courts on Sundays (Murray 1980, pp. 12-14). Though latterly no longer a member of the Methodist Connexion, Margaret Thatcher has cited with approval the views of John Wesley on economic morality.[3]

Wesleyan Methodism was treated by Weber in his essay as a late, non-Calvinist revival of ascetic Protestantism (Weber 1930, pp. 139-43). It serves, thus, as a kind of link in the historical chain between the Reformation and the contemporary world, and it will therefore be instructive to look at the economic ethic preached in Wesley's *Sermons*. Many very familiar themes are to be found there. There is, first of all, a work ethic, and an anathema against idleness and self-indulgence. 'Every man that has any pretence to be a Christian' will not fail 'to apply themselves to the *business* of their calling ... seeing that it is impossible that an idle man can be a good man: sloth being inconsistent with religion'. 'We ought to use all diligence in our calling'. Why? 'In order to owe no man anything'; 'to the end we may eat our own bread, and be burdensome to no man'; 'to provide for our [wife and] children ... the plain necessaries of life ... [but] not delicacies: not superfluities'; in general and above all, 'to please God; to do, not [our] own will, but the will of him who sent [us] into the world; ... aiming, not at ease, pleasure or riches; ... but merely at the glory of God' (Wesley 1825, Vol. II, p. 435, Vol. I, pp. 364-5, Vol. II, pp. 435-6). If Wesley's work ethic has any originality, it is his preoccupation with 'redeeming the time' from excessive sleep. He is, admittedly, less rigorous than 'that good and sensible man, Mr Baxter', who would not allow the true Christian more than four hours of sleep out of twenty-four: Wesley allows at least six for most people, but, as a general principle, 'that measure ... which nature requires, but no more'. Excessive sleep is 'a sin against God ... For we cannot waste, or (which comes to the same thing), not improve, any part of our worldly substance ... without sinning against Him' (Wesley 1825, Vol. II, pp. 473, 472, 475). The self-indulgent sleeper makes his soul a slave to bodily appetites, instead of using soul and body in the service of God.

Our aim in our callings, says Wesley, must be to serve God, not ourselves. His sermons, accordingly, contain frequent expositions of Biblical warnings against acquisition and the love of riches, against 'laying up treasures on earth'. To love riches, he explains, is to seek for more 'worldly substance [than] will procure the necessaries and conveniences of life ... whether to lay it up, or lay it out in superfluities' (Wesley 1825, Vol. II, p. 408). It might be a little surprising that Margaret Thatcher (who, in her Sermon on the Mound, explicitly proclaimed the godliness of 'abundance') should be able to cite Wesley in her support. But it is perhaps not altogether surprising, because all of Wesley's warnings against 'covetousness' and the seeking of wealth are carefully qualified. ' "The love of money", we know, "is the root of all evil"; but not the thing itself. The fault does not lie in the money, but in them that use it. It may be used ill: and what may not?' But, Wesley continues, 'it is [in itself] an excellent gift of God, answering the noblest ends', an 'excellent talent' (Wesley 1825, Vol. I, p. 625). This being so, Wesley sums up his teachings on money in three ringing imperatives, which Mrs Thatcher has cited with approval.[4] The first two are *'Gain all you can'* (by honest means, unhurtful to our souls, as with Baxter) and *'Save all you can'*. These are the rules of Christian diligence and Christian prudence. But the third rule is the rule of Christian stewardship. God has placed men in the world 'not as a proprietor, but as a steward'. To be a faithful steward means, after providing oneself and one's family with necessities, 'if there be an overplus left, as you have opportunity, do good unto all men'. The third rule of money is: *'Give all you can'*. 'By *giving all I can*, I am effectually secured from "laying up treasures upon earth" '. In a passage reminiscent of John Paget (see above, p. 82),Wesley exclaims: 'I charge you in the name of God, do not increase your substance! As it comes daily or yearly, so let it go: otherwise you "lay up treasures upon earth". And this our Lord as flatly forbids, as murder and adultery' (Wesley 1825, Vol. II, pp. 413, Vol. I, pp. 626-34, Vol. II, p. 441). We are to gain all we can, but not thereby to become any richer. In effect, it is our duty to work, mostly, for the benefit of others. After all, we may again wonder to what extent Wesley's message is congruent with the doctrines that have come to be known as 'Thatcherism'.

And yet the significance of Methodism in articulating Margaret Thatcher's economic philosophy is beyond question. This shows, not only in her own early upbringing, but in the role of Brian Griffiths, a practising Methodist and academic economist, and the author of two important books entitled *Morality and the Market-Place* and *The Creation of Wealth*. Griffiths was appointed by Mrs Thatcher in 1985 to lead her Policy Unit, has acted as one of her speech-writers, and was later made by her a Life Peer. The similarities between the published views of Griffiths and those of the Sermon on the Mound are impossible to miss. According to Griffiths, since man is made in God's image, part of his *raison d'être*, like that of his creator, is to work. 'The Christian sees his work as a vocation' (Griffiths 1982, p. 78; Griffiths 1984, p. 79). God has made the physical world for our use (Griffiths interprets the oft-cited passage in Genesis, instructing men to 'subdue' the earth, as a 'specific commission to harness the resources of the natural world for our benefit'). 'Wealth creation' is the discharge of the Divine commission, a Divine 'mandate' (Griffiths 1982, pp. 79-80, 91-2). God's intention for his world is not poverty, but prosperity (also not 'luxury', though Griffiths does not explain the difference between prosperity and luxury). Like Wesley, Griffiths invokes the Christian duty of stewardship, though in a less demanding way: 'justice demands that society should care for those who are unable adequately to look after themselves ... and in that context caring involves redistribution of income', that is, government provision of welfare services (Griffiths 1984, pp. 79-80). But Griffiths is highly critical of the British welfare state (as of 1982), which he sees as an indiscriminate handing out of money that flouts the principle of individual responsibility. Where poverty is due to misfortune, the needs of the poor should be provided; where it is due to laziness, there is no obligation to make such provision (Griffiths 1982, pp. 112-13, 96).

In spite of all this, there are great differences between the views expressed in Griffiths' book, on the one hand, and those of the Sermon on the Mound, and 'Thatcherism', on the other. In Griffiths' view, market incentives and inequalities are made necessary by man's fallen state, in other words by original sin. He repudiates the secular celebrators of the market order, 'libertarians such as Friedman and Hayek', because they are concerned only with the rights of property, not with its duties – thus he can describe himself as a supporter of the concept of the 'social market economy' (Griffiths 1984, pp. 79-80, 63). These are not 'Thatcherite' sentiments.

There is no evidence that Margaret Thatcher has read Max Weber, but it is certain that Brian Griffiths has done so,[5] and has found in the Weber Thesis a model for his own Christian (or Methodist) economic theory. To the extent that the latter found favour with her, she might be said to have been significantly, if indirectly, influenced by Weber. This, however, may be misleading. It all depends whether her Christian case for capitalism is a motive, or a rationalization of other motives. Unlike Brian Griffiths, Margaret Thatcher is well known to be an enthusiastic admirer of the free-market economic theory of Hayek,[6] which professedly derives from the liberal economic theory of Adam Smith, and Smith's name too has been invoked by her[7] (she does not, however, seem to share, or perhaps to be aware of, Smith's suspicion of the often *illiberal*, monopolistic motives of capitalist 'merchants and manufacturers',[8] which Hayek does not emphasize). It is also known that *The Wealth of Nations* was recommended or even compulsory reading for the top civil servants of her close ministerial colleague, Sir Keith Joseph.[9] However – and this is the point – it is not easy to marry consistently the two viewpoints, one of which sees 'wealth creation' as a religious duty and a part of God's universal plan, while the other sees it as the pursuit of self-interest in a way which, given the right institutions, also promotes the general good. Hayek, who is an unusually clear-sighted exponent of the latter view, is quite explicit that the distribution of economic rewards in a capitalist market has nothing whatever to do with moral desert (Hayek 1960, Chapter 6. Contrast this with the view, attributed by Weber to the adherents of the Protestant ethic, that economic success and virtue are correlated.) In the Sermon on the Mound, there is only one brief invocation of the Smith-Hayek view: the remark that there are 'some' who would not work hard without an economic incentive. 'And we need their efforts too'. This is perhaps a little disingenuous. If we need the efforts of such people (hence must offer material rewards for their efforts, and not destroy incentives by excessive taxation), it is because the 'some' are in fact the overwhelming majority. Contrary to the impression that the Sermon possibly seeks to give, the Thatcherite system is based much more on the appeal to self-interest than to religious duty. John Wesley, I suggest, would not have understood the concept of excessive taxation.

The 'Christian' and the 'Hayekian' defence of capitalism are two horses which can be ridden in harness up to a point, but only up to a point. There comes a point at which they pull apart. A crux is the Christian concept of stewardship, so much emphasized by Baxter and the Puritan writers, by Wesley, and even by Brian Griffiths. Margaret Thatcher believes, or says she believes, in the duty of Christian stewardship. The Sermon on the Mound does not use the word, but the idea is there in the endorsement of help – which in modern society must be ensured by state action – for the unfortunate, the elderly, the sick and the disabled. But this provision of state help must not be 'so great' that it destroys the sense of individual responsibility. However clear this distinction may be in theory (it is perhaps not totally clear), its application in practical politics is a veritable thicket of difficulties. Probably no practical arrangement will treat all cases as they should be, judged in terms of Mrs Thatcher's distinction. This being so, the crucial question is: which way to lean? Which is the greater evil, too much welfare, or too little? I must leave it to historians of the Thatcher government's rough treatment of the British welfare system to infer to which side she leaned. Be it noted, however, that the Hayekian view encounters little difficulty in this context, because its basic principle is just to maximize *total* wealth by maximizing economic incentives.

What the crux of stewardship tells us about the true nature of Thatcherism is not certain, because of the practical complexities involved. However, there is one simple issue where the Christian and the Hayekian justification of capitalism come into sharp, clear conflict, where the Christian's duty to his God and the capitalist's right to his profit stand in total contradiction to one another. This issue is Sabbatarianism versus freedom to trade every day of the week, including Sunday. Mrs Thatcher in power was always unequivocally in favour of free Sunday trading (though her efforts to institute it, in England and Wales, did not succeed). This may seem a surprising view for a committed, traditionalist Christian who, it has been said, 'believes in the ten commandments' (Murray 1980, p. 70). The Fourth Commandment, however, is as follows:

> Keep the sabbath day to sanctify it, as the Lord thy God hath commanded thee;
> Six days thou shalt labour, and do all thy work;
> But the seventh day is the sabbath of the Lord thy God; in it thou shalt not do any work, thou, nor thy son, nor thy daughter, nor thy manservant, nor thy maidservant, nor thine ox, nor thine ass, nor any of thy cattle, nor the stranger that is within thy gates; that thy manservant and thy maidservant may rest as well as thou.

Alderman Roberts, we recall, was a strict Sabbatarian, who would not allow his daughter Margaret even to go to the cinema or play cards on Sunday (just how *these* prohibitions are deduced from the Fourth Commandment, is not clear). Presumably he would never have dreamt of opening his shop on a Sunday. Did his daughter's later attitude to the Lord's Day make him turn in his grave?

Let us return to Weber. However important or unimportant the role of Protestant Christianity in the phenomenon called 'Thatcherism', Weber thought that 'victorious capitalism' had no further need of support from ascetic Protestant ideas, and in this he must be right, since victorious capitalism long ago extended its triumphs far beyond the limits of Protestant or even Christian civilization. In fact, the most dynamic areas of capitalist expansion have in recent times been in the Far East, in societies of more or less Confucian culture, such as South Korea, various overseas Chinese communities, and above all Japan. It is an interesting and much debated question why this is so: equally interesting is the question why these societies, now so economically dynamic, did *not* lead the way into capitalism in the first place (despite the fact that, judged simply as 'civilizations', China and

Japan were fully as advanced and prosperous as the West, probably more so, in the sixteenth and seventeenth centuries). I cannot hope to answer that question here. However, I will offer a few speculative remarks. Casual observation of contemporary Japan and the overseas Chinese communities makes it abundantly clear that these societies do not lack a work ethic. However, it is a work ethic very different from the Puritan one – it has nothing to do with pleasing God or proving the salvation of one's eternal soul (these are totally un-Confucian concepts), but is entirely secular and this-worldly. In fact it is perhaps misleading to call it a work ethic at all – it is really (the expression of) a loyalty ethic. The Japanese work ethic is, one might say, the expression of the Japanese loyalty ethic in an age of capitalism. The employee of Mitsubishi, it has been said, would die for Mitsubishi – just as, in a past century, the Forty-seven Ronin, one after another, died loyally and gloriously for the honour of their dead Lord.[10] A loyalty ethic as powerful as the Japanese is admirably suited to the needs of *already established* capitalism, especially in the era of the large corporation. It is obviously not so apt to set capitalism going, as it were by accident, in the first place. In the first place, there is nothing capitalist to be loyal to. To give birth to capitalism in the first place, an individualistic, self-reliant ethic, such as ascetic Protestantism fostered, was perhaps necessary. In the case of Japan, of course, capitalism did not begin by accident, but as a result of a deliberate government policy decision, after the Meiji Revolution.

Not only is ascetic Protestantism no longer necessary to maintain capitalist development, it is in the long run rather poorly adapted to it. The Protestant calling ethic contains an inner contradiction, latent only in the early days of capitalism, now apparent to all. As noted above, the injunction to ceaseless diligence in one's particular calling had two justifications, an ascetic and an altruistic one. Such diligence mortifies the flesh, and is also service to one's fellows. It should lead, not to self-indulgence, but to help for one's neighbour out of any surplus thus accumulated. However, as capitalism develops into a mighty productive machine, it creates far more wealth than is, on any puritan view, necessary to human existence. According to puritanism, this excess is corrupting and harmful to the soul. Puritanism can no longer be, without embarrassment, the basis of capitalistic endeavour (we noted above Brian Griffiths' attempt to justify 'prosperity' while repudiating 'luxury', without telling us what the difference is). Alternative theories are, of course, available which straightforwardly endorse a utilitarian maximization of pleasures: and on these we now act, by and large. But we are sufficiently the heirs of our Puritan past to feel uneasy and even guilty about it (as for example, the current vogue-word 'consumerism', intended as an indictment of our way of life, plainly shows). Post-Puritan capitalist civilization is inevitably gnawed by self-doubt.

Let us give the last word to Weber.

> Where the fulfilment of the calling cannot directly be related to the highest spiritual and cultural values, or when, on the other hand, it need not be felt simply as an economic compulsion, the individual generally abandons the attempt to justify it at all ... No one knows whether, at the end of this tremendous development, entirely new prophets will arise (Weber 1930, p. 182).

Indeed, no-one knows. Nor does anyone know what their prophecy might be, or whether any new prophecy can alter the course of world history.

Appendix A

THE GLASGOW CITY MOTTO – AN EPITOME OF THE WEBER THESIS?

It is tempting to describe Glasgow as the Weberian city *par excellence*. In the nineteenth century, it was known as the 'second city' of the British Empire – second in population only to London. In 1690, the city's population was under 12,000; in 1801, 77,000; by 1871, half-a-million. Glasgow's spectacular growth was entirely due to industrialization. Unlike the handful of more populous European cities in its heyday, Glasgow was not, is not, and has never been a political capital or centre of government. It was, in the first place, a small ecclesiastical city, later a huge industrial one. In between occurred the Reformation. Glasgow was the seat of a bishopric from the twelfth century, when the building of the city's cathedral was begun. In 1451, thanks to a papal Bull, the cathedral city became a cathedral-cum-university city, and thereby, more or less, a west coast equivalent of St Andrews in the east. Unlike almost all other medieval Scottish cathedrals, that of Glasgow survived the Reformation largely intact, being simply made over to the new religion: the university, however, was 're-founded' by Andrew Melville in 1577, in order to purge it of Popery.

As Glasgow developed over the centuries from a small, ecclesiastical, Papist city to a large and predominantly Protestant one, it adopted a series of official coats of arms, and accompanying mottoes. The sequence of mottoes is of great interest. The present-day motto is 'Let Glasgow Flourish', and can be seen on the city's armorial bearings, which were designed by Andrew MacGeorge and confirmed by the Lord Lyon King of Arms in 1866. The apparently quite secular nature of the motto is, however, misleading, or rather, conceals a history. 'Let Glasgow Flourish' is an abbreviated version of a longer invocation which at first represented a union of the municipal and the ecclesiastical, namely: 'Lord, Let Glasgow Flourish Through The Preaching Of Thy Word And Praising Thy Name'. These words are first to be found, surrounding the motifs of the City

Corporation's armorial bearings, on the steeple bell of Glasgow's Tron Church, cast, by order of the city magistrates, in 1631, at a time when the official common seal of the Burgh of Glasgow combined these motifs with a quite different legend, in Latin: 'Sigillum Comune Civitatis Glasguae' (which simply means 'The common seal of the City of Glasgow', and had been in use since medieval times). The form of words which would become the present city motto began to be abbreviated as early as 1663: a woodcut in a New Testament of that date, printed by the Town Printer and reprinted in 1670, has the arms surrounded by the words 'Lord Let Glasgow Flourish By The Preaching Of Thy Word'. John McUre's *History of Glasgow*, published in 1736, printed an ornate version of the arms with the motto reduced to the three words 'Let Glasgow Flourish'. But not until 1789 were these words incorporated into the city's official common seal, together with an English translation of the old Latin wording: 'The Common Seal Of The City of Glasgow'. In the version finally approved by the Lord Lyon in 1866, these words were dropped, leaving the now familiar 'Let Glasgow Flourish' in sole possession. In brief, the post-Reformation religious invocation was first abbreviated, then merged with the city's common seal, and finally became recognized as its official municipal motto in the abbreviated, one might say secularized form. Glasgow's flourishing, it seems, had lost the explicit connection with Protestant piety on which it had at first been seen to depend. Some sort of 'spirit of capitalism' had emerged from, and discarded, a 'Protestant ethic'.

The reader may be interested to see the visual evidence of all this. I therefore reproduce below seven illustrations, the first six of which are copied from MacGeorge's *Inquiry as to the Armorial Insignia of the City of Glasgow*[1]:

Figure 1:   The Glasgow Burgh seal of 1325
Figure 2:   The Glasgow Burgh seal of 1647
Figure 3:   The arms and motto on the steeple bell of the Tron Church, 1631
Figure 4:   The arms and motto in the Town Printer's New Testament of 1663 and 1670
Figure 5:   The arms and motto in McUre's *History of Glasgow*, 1736
Figure 6:   The Glasgow Burgh seal of 1789
Figure 7:   The modern official armorial bearings and motto of the City of Glasgow, as patented by the Lord Lyon King of Arms in 1866

FIGURE 1

FIGURE 2

FIGURE 3

FIGURE 4

FIGURE 5

FIGURE 6

FIGURE 7

Appendix B

LIST OF PROTESTANT CATECHISMS THAT DISCUSS THE DECALOGUE'S COMMANDMENT AGAINST STEALING (EITHER EXPLICITLY, OR WITHIN A GENERAL DISCUSSION OF THE SECOND TABLE)

Richard Allein: *A Brief Explanation of the Common Catechism* (2nd ed., 1631)

William Ames: *The Chief Heads of Divinity, Briefly and Orderly Set Down* (1612)

William Attersoll: *The Principles of Christian Religion* (1635)

Samuel Austin: *A Practical Catechism* (1647)

I.B.: *A Breviate of Saving Knowledge* (1643)

John Ball: *A Short Catechism* (13th ed., 1630)

John Ball: *A Short Treatise containing all the Principal Grounds of the Christian Religion* (expanded version of the preceding) (1631)

John Ball (of Langton in Purbeck): *Short Questions and Answers, Explaining the common catechism in the Book of Common Prayer* (1638)

Richard Bernard: *The Common Catechism, with a Commentary* (6th ed., 1632)

Richard Bernard: *The Larger Catechism* (1625)

Samuel Brown: *The Sum of Christian Religion* (1630)

Francis Bunney: *A Guide unto Godliness* (1617)

R.C. (Richard Greenham): *A Brief and Necessary Catechism* (1602)

T.C. (probably Thomas Cartwright): *A Treatise of Christian Religion* (1616)

John Calvin: *The Geneva Catechism* (1594)

John Carpenter: *Contemplations for the Institution of Christian Religion* (1601)

John Cotton: *Milk for Babes, drawn out of the breasts of both Testaments* (1646)

Richard Cox: *A Short Catechism* (1620)
John Craig: *A Short Sum of the Whole Catechism* (1581)
Thomas Cranmer: *Book of Common Prayer* (1549)
William Crashaw: *Milk for Babes, or a North Country Catechism* (4th imp., 1622)
Stephen Denison: *A Compendious Catechism* (7th imp., 1632)
Edward Dering: *A Short Catechism for Householders* (1580)
John Dod and Richard Cleaver: *A Plain and Familiar Exposition of the Ten Commandments, with a Methodical Short Catechism* (1607)
Edward Elton: *A Form of Catechizing* (1629)
M. Fountaine: *A Catechism and plain instruction for children ... written in French ... and translated into English by T.W.* (n.d.)
Alexander Gee: *The Ground of Christianity* (1584)
William Gouge: *A Short Catechism* (8th ed., 1636)
Thomas Granger: *The Tree of Good and Evil* (1616)
Richard Greenham: see R.C.
G.G. (George Gyffard): *A Catechism containing the sum of Christian Religion* (1583)
Robert Horn: *Points of Instruction for the Ignorant* (1613)
W. Horne: *A Christian Exercise* (n.d.)
Richard Jones: *A Brief and Necessary Catechism* (1609)
Martin Luther: *A Short Catechism for the Use of Ordinary Pastors and Preachers* (otherwise *The Short Catechism*) (1529)
Martin Luther: *The Greater Catechism* (1530)
J. Mayer: *A Short Catechism* (1646)
John Mayer: *The English Catechism* (1621)
John Mico: *Milk for the Younger, or a Catechism for the Younger Sort* and *Meat for the Stronger, or a Catechism for the Elder Sort* (4th ed., 1631)
Josias Nichols: *An Order of Household Instruction* (1596)
Martin Nichols: *A Catechism* (1631)
John Norton: *A Brief and Excellent Treatise containing the Doctrine of Godliness* (1647)
Alexander Nowell: *A Catechism, or First Instruction and Learning of Christian Religion* (1570)
Alexander Nowell: *A Catechism, or Institution of Christian Learning* (1577)
Richard Openshaw: *Short Questions and Answers, containing the Sum of Christian Religion* (1584, 1633)
John Paget: *A Primer of Christian Religion* (1601)

Herbert Palmer: *An Endeavour of Making the Principles of Christian Religion ... plain and easy* (4th imp., 1644)

Thomas Pearston: *A Short Instruction unto Christian Religion* (1590)

William Perkins: *The Foundation of Christian Religion Gathered into Six Principles* (1590)

Edmund Reeve: *The Communion Book Catechism Expounded* (1635)

Ezekiel Rogers: *The Chief Grounds of Christian Religion* (1642)

Samuel Rutherford: *Ane Catechism containing the sum of Christian Religion* (unpublished)

S.S.: *A Brief Instruction for all Families* (1583)

Christopher Shutte: *A Compendious Form and Sum of Christian Doctrine* (1581, 1637)

John Stallholm: *A Catechism for Children in Years, and Children in Understanding* (1644)

John Stockwood: *A Short Catechism for Householders* (1583)

William Twisse: *A Brief Catechetical Exposition of Christian Doctrine* (1633)

Zacharias Ursinus and Casper Olevianus: *The Heidelberg Catechism*

James Ussher: *Principles of Christian Religion* (1644)

James Ussher: *A Body of Divinity* (1645)

Henry Vesey: *The Scope of Scripture* (1633)

Matthew Virell: *A Learned and Excellent Treatise containing all the principal grounds of Christian Religion* (1594)

William Ward: *Short Grounds of Catechism* (1627)

Richard Webb: *A Key of Knowledge for Catechizing Children in Christ* (1622)

George Webbe: *A Brief Exposition of the Principles of Christian Religion* (1612)

William Whitaker: *A Short Sum of Christianity* (1630)

Josias White: *A Plain and Familiar Exposition upon the Creed, X Commandments, Lord's Prayer and Sacraments* (7th ed., 1632)

Henry Wilkinson: *A Catechism* (3rd ed., 1629)

Thomas Wilson: *Saints by Calling, or Called to be Saints* (1620)

Thomas Wolfall: *Children's Bread ...* (1646)

Thomas Wyllie: *A Catechism* (n.d.)

John Yates: *A Short and Brief Sum of Saving Knowledge* (1621)

John Yates: *A Model of Divinity* (1622)

Anonymous catechisms

A Form of Catechizing in True Religion (1581)

The Principles of the true Christian Religion (1590)

A Catechism, or brief instruction in the Principles and Grounds of the Christian Religion (1617)

A Catechism of Christian Religion, allowed to be taught in the Churches and Schools within the County Palatine (1617)

The Elements of the Beginning of the Oracles of God (1619)

A Brief Dialogue, concerning preparation for the worthy receiving of the Lord's Supper, taken, for the most part, out of the ten sermons of Mr Dod and Mr Clever (1633)

A Catechism, or Institution of Christian Religion (1638)

A Pattern of Catechistical Doctrine ... and the whole Decalogue succinctly and judiciously expounded (1641) (possibly by Archbishop Ussher)

The New Catechism according to the form of the Kirk of Scotland (1644)

Notes

Chapter 1

1. One of the leaders of English Puritanism in the Civil War period, the Independent John Goodwin, is described by Harrison (1937, p. 142) as Arminian in theology. According to Spurr (1991, pp. 314-315), there was never a time when all Puritans were Calvinists. He asserts that, before 1700, full-blown Arminianism had established itself at the very heart of Presbyterianism in England.

2. White quotes Bishop Joseph Hall's view on the matter that there was no need for 'the souls of quiet Christians to be racked with subtler questions' (1626). On a similar tack, King Charles I 'would not have this high point meddled with withall or debated, because it was too high for the people's understanding, and other points which concern reformation and newness of life were more needful and profitable'. After the Restoration, says Spurr, English churchmen rejected 'those hard disputes about God's eternal decrees, and strange workings of his grace, which will never cease, and never be decided', and on which, as Sir Henry Yelverton put it in 1670, 'learned and good men may differ'. Yelverton added that 'the church's peace ought not to be disturbed with such unnecessary determinations'.

3. Robertson, 1933, has argued at length that there is no significant difference in the economic ethic of Post-Reformation Catholics and Protestants.

Chapter 2

1. This phenomenon is called, not quite accurately, 'The Weberian revolution of the High Middle Ages' by Randall Collins in Collins 1986, pp. 52-4.

2. I owe this information to my friend and colleague John Fowler.

3. At times, Weber himself pointed to the tensions between monastic asceticism and the worldly success it created, for example in Weber 1930, p. 174, and Weber 1948, pp. 331-2.

4. Aquinas' acceptance of the merchant's role was, nevertheless, hardly enthusiastic. While admitting the necessity of his social function, Aquinas still considered it to have about it 'something sordid and shameful' (cf. Gurevich 1990, p. 247).

Chapter 3

1. An important book on the Weber Thesis in relation to Scotland is Marshall 1980.
2. Robertson, 1933, argues that Weber's case for the novelty of Luther's use of the conception of the calling is unconvincing (p. 4). His argument is, however, itself unconvincing. For example, terms such as the French 'office' do not, contrary to Robertson, have the same significance as the term 'calling' or 'Beruf'.
3. The words are from 2 Peter 1:10.
4. On Rollock, see Marshall 1980, pp. 66-73.
5. For Weber's methodology of ideal types, see Weber 1949, pp. 89-105. He is explicit as to his use of the methodology in relation to the Weber Thesis – cf. Weber 1930, p. 98.
6. An important example is William Ames, who is particularly insistent not only that men may certainly know whether they are in a state of grace, but that it is their absolute duty to enquire into this state 'with all diligence possible'. On the one hand, a man who has received the Holy Ghost, if he 'should, at any time, by a sudden temptation, defile himself with sin ... he shall find such *strugglings* and *strivings* within himself, that he is never quiet until his filthiness is washed off ...' (Ames 1652, p. 25). On the other hand, 'We are assured of the grace of God (by the witness of the Spirit), not only for the present, but also for the continuance of it, to the doing of every good work' (Ames 1639, p. 37).
7. No one who has studied the sources can doubt the intense preoccupation among members of the Reformed churches, including laymen, with the problem of 'assurance' as to one's state of grace. On this see Kendall 1981, and Jensen 1979, pp. 174-224. Also of considerable interest in this regard are some of the writings of John Knox, for example, 'A Fort for the Afflicted' and 'Letters to his Mother-in-Law' (Knox 1845).
8. The classic literary expression of the antinomianism latent in Calvinism is James Hogg, *The Private Memories and Confessions of a Justified Sinner*.
9. Cf. Haller 1957, Chapter III, especially pp. 83-9 on this point.

10. The Confession is quoted from John Knox's *History of the Reformation in Scotland*, Vol. II ed. W. Croft Dickinson (Nelson, Edinburgh 1949).
11. The early Lutherans saw no such contradiction, because their conception of confession and atonement was not, unlike the pre-Reformation one, linked to penance, hence was not dependent on 'works'. Nevertheless absolution by or through another person is not salvation by faith. Cf. Lea 1896, p. 515.
12. This might account for the statistics, reported in the notes to the first chapter of *The Protestant Ethic and the Spirit of Capitalism*, suggesting markedly greater economic success by (Lutheran) Protestants than Catholics in Baden and other German states (Weber 1930, pp. 188-9) – statistics which do not chime well with Weber's remarks on Luther and Lutheranism in Chapter III.

Chapter 4

1. According to Weber, the Calvinists prescribed intense worldly activity as a means to assurance of election. 'It and it alone disperses religious doubts and gives the certainty of grace' (Weber 1930 p. 112). Later, he notes that Baxter, for whom (typically) this worldly activity must take the form of a useful calling, adopted the 'private profitableness' of the calling as a measure of its social, moral and religious worth (Weber 1930, p. 162).
2. Mandy Rice-Davies was a leading figure in a celebrated call-girl scandal that rocked the British political establishment in the last years of Harold Macmillan's premiership. The words in question, which have entered into folklore, were her response to a prominent person's denial of misbehaviour: 'Well, he would say that, wouldn't he?'
3. 'Godliness is profitable unto all things, having promise of the life that now is, and of that which is to come' (1 Timothy 4:8); 'The hand of the diligent maketh rich' (Proverbs 10:4, Authorised Version).
4. The theme is a very frequent one. Here are some more examples: 'The reprobate ... in prosperity are so puffed up that they forget God' (Knox 1845, p. 109); 'The rich and proud are under a constant temptation to live idly' (Baxter 1673, p. 454); it is 'a mark of the wicked' to be 'debauched by their prosperity' (Hutcheson 1669, p. 164).
5. A notable example is Robertson 1933, pp. 7-14.

6. 'The mercy of men's temporal enjoyments consists not so much in their enjoying them, as in their being satisfied and contented with their lot' (Hutcheson 1669, p. 394); 'If ye will be persuaded to be Christians indeed, ye shall have the outward things ye have need of ... And for superfluities, what need ye care for them?' (Binning 1839, Vol. III, p. 344). Hutcheson and Binning are both Scots.

7. Examples of this theme may be found in Dod and Cleaver 1606, Ch. 10, p. 94; Steele 1825, p. 29; Abernethy 1622, p. 378; Durham 1676, p. 249.

8. Anthony Tuckney has an interesting discussion of the temporal promises. Like Calvin, he points out that 'if Godliness ... have the promise of this life as well as that which is to come, it will be the more desirable'. But his view is that it was 'in the nonage of the Church' that 'God used to promise [outward riches] to his children, and by them to train them up to obedience' (Tuckney 1676, p. 167). Nowadays, he implies, Christians should look for a spiritual inheritance.

9. Cf. also Dickson 1651, pp. 68, 70; Durham 1759, p. 326; Colvill 1673, pp. 143, 145.

10. Some passages that stress the right *use* of wealth rather than *limits* on wealth are the following: 'Though no man can serve God and riches, yet he may serve God with riches ... He may seek both, in order one to another, namely God for himself, riches not for himself but for God' (Taylor 1653, p. 477); 'Worldly things must be so craved, as we first give them to God' (Greenham 1605, p. 432); 'Seeking after money is wrong [when] our affection is sinful, as if we seek it only for itself, that we may be rich, or to bestow it on our lusts' (Preston 1641, p. 247). Preston, however, adds that 'When we seek thus, we seek it in excess', and also preaches against covetousness in the sense of desiring excessive 'measure' of wealth.

11. The words 'steward' and 'stewardship' do not occur in the index of the English translation of Weber's *The Protestant Ethic and the Spirit of Capitalism* (Weber 1930). So far as I know they occur only once in the text, in the following passage, which applies the idea only in a modern context, and in a highly pejorative sense: thanks to 'the influence of Puritanism ... the toleration of pleasure in cultural goods ... always ran up against one characteristic limitation: they must not cost anything. Man is only a trustee of the goods which have come to him through God's grace ... The idea of a man's duty to his possessions, to which he subordinates

himself as an obedient steward, or even as an acquisitive machine, bears with chilling weight upon his life' (Weber 1930, p. 170).
12. The theme of man's obligation to serve God is pervasive in Puritan and Calvinist literature, often but not always linked to the idea of the calling. Frequently quoted is the Biblical passage: 'Be not slothful in business, but fervent in spirit, serving the Lord' (Romans, 12:11) – see, for example, Durham 1676, p. 187.

Chapter 5

1. The importance of catechisms has been underlined by a leading historian of the post-Reformation period in England in the following words: 'No student of the religious mentality of the age, or the dissemination of protestantism, can afford to neglect these often skilfully composed summaries of Christian doctrine' (Collinson 1982, p. 232).
2. This information is drawn from Alexander Law, *Schoolbooks of Old Scotland, 1700-1900*, Ch. 2, which, thanks to the kindness of the author, I was able to consult in typescript prior to publication.
3. Gunn is cited in Alexander Law, *op. cit.*
4. The version of Calvin's catechism quoted is an English translation of 1594, published by Richard Schilders of Middelburgh, Zeeland. Spelling has been modernized in this and subsequent quotations from old texts.
5. Other catechisms which give the same rule of interpretation include Carpenter 1601, Brown 1630, Parr 1614, Norton 1647, Nichols 1596, Fountaine's *Catechism and Plain Instruction for Children* ... (n.d.), and two anonymous catechisms: *A Brief and Short Catechism necessary for all them that would be Christians* (n.d.), and *Short Principles of Religion* (1644).
6. The same is true of Nowell's more advanced catechism, called *A Catechism, or First Instruction and Learning of Christian Religion*.
7. Or presumably so, in a few cases which bear no date.
8. The pre-Reformation catechism is Dietrich Kolde's widely used *Faithful Mirror or Small Handbook for Christians* (See D. Janz, *Three Reformation Catechisms*, New York and Toronto: Edwin Mellen Press, 1982. Kolde's catechism was first published in 1470 in Cologne). The others are the Catechism of the Council of Trent, the Catechism of Archbishop Hamilton (St Andrews, 1551), Peter Canisius' *Catechism or Short Instruction of Christian*

Religion, and two English recusant catechisms by Laurence Vaux and William Warford. Erasmus' *Plain and Godly Exposition ... of the common creed ... and of the ten commandments* (not strictly a catechism) also makes no mention of a duty to seek wealth in its discussion of the commandment against stealing.

9. A complete list of Protestant catechisms is given in Appendix B. Of the 'ten', almost all are mentioned in the text of this chapter: another important example is *A Brief Dialogue ... taken, for the most part, out of the ten sermons of Mr L. Dod and Mr Clever* (1633).

10. Alexander Mitchell asserts (Mitchell 1886, p. ix) that 'at least twelve or fourteen' of them were in this category, and then gives a list of eleven names (not including Good and Rutherford) of Assemblymen who were definitely catechists. I believe two names in Mitchell's list (Cawdrey and Byfield) are erroneous (probably due to different authors having the same surname, the clerical office tending to run in families). I have not yet been able to read the catechism of Obadiah Sedgewick.

11. On Rutherford's role, see Mitchell 1886, pp. xxvii, xxxiv-v. Mitchell thinks that Rutherford prepared his catechism in the hope that the Assembly's committee would adopt it.

12. According to Alexander Mitchell, Josias White was the elder brother of the Assemblyman John White. This catechism is credited to both brothers, but in Mitchell's view John is probably the author, Josias the copyist (Mitchell 1886, p. xlviii).

13. See the entry on Ussher in the *Dictionary of National Biography*.

14. Mitchell later realised that 'M.N.' might be Nichols rather than Newcomen (see Mitchell 1886, p. xviii).

15. See the *Short-Title Catalogue of English Books, 1475-1640*.

16. Not to be confused with another contemporary John Ball, also the author of a catechism, who was minister at Langton in Purbeck, Dorset. *The Short-Title of English Books, 1475-1640* fails to distinguish the two.

17. According to Wing's *Short-Title Catalogue, 1641-1700*.

18. For the joint attributions, see the *Short Title Catalogue of English Books, 1475-1640*.

19. For example, by J. Sears McGee, *The Godly Man in Stuart England* (New Haven, Yale U.P., 1976).

20. This work contains three catechisms, including *Milk for the Younger, or a Catechism for the Younger Sort*, and *Meat for the Stronger, or a Catechism for the Elder Sort*.

21. Austin is probably following the catechism of William Perkins, *op. cit.*, which uses a similar formula.
22. The precise figure depends on interpretation. My figure of 39 includes two which do not relate charity particularly to the commandment against stealing.
23. My figure includes one catechism that mentions the importance of the calling but not (explicitly) of work therein. It excludes five catechisms which enjoin diligence, etc., but do not explicitly discuss the ten commandments.
24. This catechism was already in print in 1580, and still in print in 1631.
25. According to the DNB, Paget, after being ejected for nonconformity, went to Holland in 1604, and became in 1607 minister of the English Presbyterian church in Amsterdam. He retired in 1637, and died three years later.

Chapter 6

1. See for example Dunn 1968, Parts IV and V, and O'Neill 1981.
2. Flavell is the author of a much-read *Exposition of the Assembly's Catechism*. See Flavell 1701.
3. Letter of William Paterson to Principal Dunlop dated March 29, 1698, in *Letters from Darien*, n.d., p. 211.
4. *The Darien Papers 1695-1700* (Edinburgh, 1849), p. 261.
5. *A Letter from the Commission of the General Assembly of the Church of Scotland, met at Glasgow, July 2nd, 1699 to the Honourable Council, and Inhabitants of the Scots Colony of Caledonia in America* (Edinburgh) pp. 8-10, 14.
6. *The Darien Papers 1695-1700* (Edinburgh 1849), p. 271.
7. *Principles of Trade* was written jointly with George Whatley.
8. William Ames listed, among 'things ... required for due exercising an honest calling', 'wisdom in observing, taking and using rightly opportunity' (Ames 1639, Fourth Book, pp. 250-1). According to the Scot George Hutcheson, 'The Lord ... hath appointed times and opportunities of [men's] callings which are not to be neglected ... A man that followeth a calling from God, and improveth all the opportunities thereof, is in a safe course' (Hutcheson 1657, p. 213). Neither explains what he means by 'opportunity' or 'opportunities', so one can only wonder whether the terms bespeak a conflation of religion and business enterprise.

Chapter 7

1. The text of the Sermon is printed in *The Observer*, 22nd May 1988, pp. 1-2.
2. The right use of wealth is, of course, the doctrine of stewardship, not explicitly invoked in the Sermon on the Mound. It has, however, been invoked elsewhere by Margaret Thatcher: creating wealth, she has said, is a Christian obligation 'if we are to fulfil our role as stewards of the resources and talents the Creator has provided for us' (Thatcher 1989, p. 126, cited in Keat and Abercrombie 1991, p. 25).
3. '[Wesley] inculcated the work ethic, and duty. You worked hard, you got on by the result of your own efforts. Then, as you prospered, it was your duty to help others to prosper also. The essence of Methodism is the Parable of the Talents' (Margaret Thatcher, quoted in Young 1989, p. 420).
4. See 'Mrs Thatcher's Sayings of the Decade', *The Observer*, 30th April 1989, p. 13.
5. For references to Weber, see Griffiths 1982, p. 140, and Griffiths 1984, pp. 29-30.
6. Laudatory references to Hayek can be found in Thatcher 1977, pp. 26, 66, 72, 91, 114. The influence of Hayek on Margaret Thatcher's thinking is also documented in Minogue and Biddiss 1987, p. 6, and in Young and Sloman 1986, in comments by James Prior, Peter Shore, and Alfred Sherman.
7. In an interview broadcast on Radio Scotland on 24th October 1993, Mrs Thatcher said, referring to 'the policies which we pursued', that 'I got them all from Adam Smith'. She also refers to Smith as 'the greatest exponent of free enterprise economics until Hayek and Friedman' in Thatcher 1993, p. 618.
8. Smith emphasized the interest of manufacturers and merchants in excluding competition. By so doing, he says, they 'levy, for their own benefit, an absurd tax on the rest of their fellow-citizens'. Their proposals 'ought always to be listened to ... with the most suspicious attention', for they 'have generally an interest to deceive the public and ... have, upon many occasions, deceived and oppressed it' (Smith 1961, Vol. I, pp. 277-8).
9. See Halcrow 1989, pp. 135-7. Keith Joseph's influence on Margaret Thatcher is a leading theme of the book. His admiration for Adam Smith is explicit in Joseph 1976, pp. 55 and 59.
10. The remark about Mitsubishi was made on a BBC radio programme about Japan by, if I remember rightly, the American

authority on Japanese culture and society, Edwin Reischauer. The Forty-seven Ronin were feudal retainers (samurai) whose lord was humiliated and thereby forced to commit suicide in 1701. The Ronin swore and took vengeance, and then committed *harakiri*. Their grave remains a centre of pilgrimage to this day. The story of the Forty-seven Ronin is the subject of one of the most popular Japanese plays, and of innumerable woodblock prints. (I am indebted for these details to Mr Hugh Stevenson of Kelvingrove Museum and Art Gallery, Glasgow.)

Note to Appendix

1.   See MacGeorge 1866, pp. 104, 111, 129, 133, 140.

General Bibliography

Abernethy, J. (1622), *A Christian and Heavenly Treatise*, London.

Ames, William (1612), *The Chief Heads of Divinity, Briefly and Orderly Set Down*.

Ames, William (1639), *Conscience*.

Ames, William (1652), *The Saint's Security against Seducing Spirits*, London.

Austin, Samuel (1647), *A Practical Catechism*.

Ball, John (1630) (13th ed.), *A Short Catechism*.

Ball, John (1631), *A Short Treatise containing all the Principal Grounds of the Christian Religion* (8th impression), London.

Ball, John (1631), *A Treatise of Faith*, London.

Bangs, Carl (1971), *Arminius*, Abingdon Press, Nashville and New York.

Baxter, Richard (1673), *Christian Directory*.

Bayley, Lewis (n.d.), *The Practice of Piety*, Amsterdam.

Berthold von Regensburg (1862), *Vollständige Ausgabe Seiner Predigten, Erster Band*, Wilhelm Braumüller, Vienna.

Brook, Benjamin (1813), *The Lives of the Puritans* (Vol. II), London.

Brown, Samuel (1630), *The Sum of Christian Religion*.

Burke, Peter (1974), *Venice and Amsterdam: A Study of Seventeenth Century Elites*, Temple Smith, London.

Calvin, John (1594), *The Geneva Catechism*, Richard Schilders, Middelburgh.

Calvin, John (1813), *Institutes of the Christian Religion*, London.

Calvin, John (1843), *Commentaries, Vol. V: Commentary on the Book of Psalms*, Edinburgh.

Calvin, John (1961), *Commentaries: Romans, Thessalonians I and II*, Edinburgh.

Calvin, John (1972), *Commentaries: A Harmony of the Gospels, Matthew, Mark, Luke* (Vol. II), St Andrew's Press, Edinburgh.

Calvin, John (1968), 'Reply to Sadoleto' in Hillerbrand, H.J. (ed.), *The Protestant Reformation*, Harper & Row, New York.

Canisius, Peter (1588), *Ane Catechism or Short Instruction of Christian Religion*, Paris.

Carpenter, John (1601), *Contemplations for the Institution of Christian Religion*.

Carruthers, S.W. (1957), *Three Centuries of the Westminster Shorter Catechism*, University of New Brunswick, New Brunswick.

Clark, James (1701), *The Spiritual-Merchant: or, The Art of Merchandizing Spiritualized*, Glasgow.

Cockburn, John (1686), *Jacob's Vow*, Edinburgh.

Collins, Randall (1986), *Weberian Social Theory*, Cambridge University Press, Cambridge.

Collinson, Patrick (1982), *The Religion of Protestants: The Church in English Society*, Clarendon Press, Oxford.

Colvill, William (1673), *The Righteous Branch Growing out of the Root of Jesse*, Edinburgh.

Cotton, John (1641), *The Way of Life, or God's Way and Course*, London.

Cotton, John (1985), 'Christ the Fountain of Life' in Heimert, A. and Delbanco, A. (eds.), *The Puritans in America, A Narrative Anthology*, Harvard University Press.

Cremeans, Charles D. (1949), *The Reception of Calvinistic Thought in England*, University of Illinois Press, Urbana.

The Darien Papers, 1695-1700 (1849), Edinburgh.

Davidson, Donald (1980), *Essays on Actions and Events*, Clarendon Press, Oxford.

Defoe, Daniel (1726), *The Complete English Tradesman* (Vol. I), London.

Defoe, Daniel (1727), *The Complete English Tradesman* (Vol. II), London.

Denison, Stephen (1632), *A Compendious Catechism* (7th impression).

Dent, Arthur (1601), *The Plain Man's Path-way to Heaven*.

Dickson, D. (1651), *A Brief Exposition of the Evangel of Jesus Christ according to Matthew*, London.

Dod, John and Cleaver, Richard (1606 and 1611), *Proverbs*.

Dod, John and Cleaver, Richard (1607), *A Plain and Familiar Exposition of the Ten Commandments*.

Doulye, George (pseudonym of William Warford) (1604), *A Brief Instruction, by Way of Dialogue, concerning the Principal Points of Christian Religion*.

Dunn, John (1968), *The Political Thought of John Locke*, Cambridge University Press, Cambridge.

Durbin, Lynn Diane (1987), *Education by Catechism: Development of the Sixteenth Century English Catechism*. (A dissertation submitted to Northwestern University, Evanston for the degree of Doctor of Philosophy.)

Durham, James (1676), *The Law Unsealed, or a Practical Exposition of the Ten Commandments*, Glasgow.

Durham, James (1685), *Heaven on Earth*, Edinburgh.

Durham, James (1759), *An Exposition of the Whole Book of Job*, Glasgow.

Erasmus, Desiderius (1533), *Plain and Godly Exposition ... of the common creed ... and of the ten commandments*.

Flavell, John (1701), *Whole Works* (Vol. II), (includes *An Exposition of the Assembly's Catechism*), London.

Fountaine, M. (n.d.), *A Catechism and plain instruction for children*.

Franklin, Benjamin (1882), *Works*, Vol. II, London.

Franklin, Benjamin (1924), *Autobiography* (includes 'The Way to Wealth' as Appendix III), Oxford University Press, London.

Free Church of Scotland (1973), *Confession of Faith and Subordinate Standards* (includes the Larger Catechism and the Shorter Catechism of the Westminster Assembly), William Blackwood, Edinburgh.

Froude, J.A. (1865), *The Influence of the Reformation on the Scottish Character*, Edinburgh.

Gouge, William (1636), *A Short Catechism* (8th ed.).

Gray, Andrew (1839), *Works*.

Green, Ian (1986), 'For Children in Yeares and Children in Understanding: The Emergence of the English Catechism under Elizabeth and the Early Stuarts', *Journal of Ecclesiastical History* 37.

Greenham, Richard (R.C.) (1602), *A Brief and Necessary Catechism*.

Greenham, Richard (1605), *Works* (4th ed.).

Griffiths, Brian (1982), *Morality and the Market Place*, Hodder & Stoughton, London.

Griffiths, Brian (1984), *The Creation of Wealth*, Hodder & Stoughton, London.

Gurevich, A.J. (1985), *Categories of Medieval Culture*, Routledge & Kegan Paul, London.

Gurevich, A.J. (1990), 'The Merchant' in Le Goff, Jacques (ed.), *Medieval Callings*, University of Chicago Press, Chicago.

Halcrow, Morrison (1989), *Keith Joseph*, Macmillan, London.
Haley, K.H.D. (1972), *The Dutch in the Seventeenth Century*, Thames & Hudson, London.
Haller, William (1957), *The Rise of Puritanism*, Harper & Row, New York.
Hamilton, Archbishop (1882), *The Catechism Set Forth by Archbishop Hamilton, printed at St. Andrews, 1551*, William Paterson, Edinburgh.
Harrison, A.W. (1937), *Arminianism*, Duckworth, London.
Hayek, F.A. (1960), *The Constitution of Liberty*, Routledge & Kegan Paul, London.
Hill, Christopher (1958), *Puritanism and Revolution*, Secker & Warburg, London.
Hill, Christopher (1961), 'Protestantism and the Rise of Capitalism' in Fisher, F.J. (ed.), *Essays in the Economic and Social History of Tudor and Stuart England*, Cambridge University Press, Cambridge.
Hill, Christopher (1964), *Society and Puritanism in Pre-Revolutionary England*, Secker & Warburg, London.
Hogg, James, *The Private Memories and Confessions of a Justified Sinner*.
Hutcheson, G. (1657), *An Exposition of the Gospel of Jesus Christ according to John*, Ralph Smith, London.
Hutcheson, G. (1669), *An Exposition of the Book of Job*, London.
Hutchison, Margarita P. (1984), *Social and Religious Change: The Case of the English Catechism, 1560-1640*. (Dissertation submitted to the Department of History and the Committee on Graduate Studies of Stanford University, UMI.)
Hyma, Albert (1959), 'The Economic Views of the Protestant Reformers' in Green, Robert W. (ed.), *Protestantism and Capitalism*, D.C. Heath & Co., Boston.
Hyma, Albert (1967), 'A Case Study: Calvinism and Capitalism in the Netherlands, 1555-1700' in Kitch, M.J. (ed.), *Capitalism and the Reformation*, Longman, London.
Janeway, James (1676), *A Supplement to the Morning-Exercise at Cripplegate* (2nd ed.).
Janeway, James (1847), *Heaven upon Earth*, Nelson, London.
Janz, Denis (1982), *Three Reformation Catechisms: Catholic, Anabaptist, Lutheran* (Edwin Mellen Press, New York and Toronto).

Jensen, Peter F. (1979), *The Life of Faith in the Teaching of Elizabethan Protestants.* (A thesis submitted to the University of Oxford in fulfilment of the requirements for the degree of Doctor of Philosophy.)

Joseph, Keith (1976), *Stranded on the Middle Ground*, Centre for Policy Studies, London.

Keat, R. & Abercrombie, N. (1991), *Enterprise Culture*, Routledge & Kegan Paul, London.

Kendall, R.T. (1981), *Calvin and English Calvinism to 1649*, Oxford University Press, Oxford.

Knappen, M.M. (1939), *Tudor Puritanism*, University of Chicago Press, Chicago.

Knox, John (1845), *Selected Practical Writings*, Edinburgh.

Knox, John (1949), *John Knox's History of the Reformation in Scotland* (Vol. II), ed.W. Croft Dickinson, Nelson, Edinburgh.

Lawrence, C.H. (1984), *Medieval Monasticism*, Longman, London.

Lea, Henry Charles (1896), *A History of Auricular Confession and Indulgences in the Latin Church, Vol. I: Confession and Absolution*, Swann, Sonnenschein & Co., London.

Le Goff, Jacques (1988), *Your Money or Your Life*, Zone Books, New York.

Little, Lester K. (1978), *Religious Poverty and the Profit Economy in Medieval Europe*, Paul Elek, London.

Locke, John (1966), *The Second Treatise of Government and A Letter Concerning Toleration*, Basil Blackwell, Oxford.

Luther, Martin (1896), *Primary Works*, Hodder & Stoughton, London.

Luther, Martin (1961), *Works* (Vol. III), ed. J. Pelikan, Concordia Publishing House, St. Louis.

Luther, Martin (1963), *Works* (Vol. XXVI), ed. J. Pelikan, Concordia Publishing House, St. Louis.

Luther, Martin (1968), 'Commentary on St. Paul's Epistle to the Galations' in Hillerbrand, H.J. (ed.), *The Protestant Reformation*, Harper & Row, New York.

MacAlister, Sir Donald (1925), *The English Authors of the Shorter Catechism*, Maclehose, Jackson & Co., Glasgow.

McBey, James (1977), *The Early Life of James McBey*, Oxford University Press, Oxford.

McGee, J. Sears (1976), *The Godly Man in Stuart England*, Yale University Press, New Haven.

MacGeorge, Andrew (1866), *An Inquiry as to the Armorial Insignia of the City of Glasgow*, Glasgow.

McGrath, Alister E. (1990), *A Life of John Calvin*, Blackwell, Oxford.
Marshall, Gordon (1980), *Presbyteries and Profits*, Clarendon Press, Oxford.
Mico, John (1631), *Spiritual Food and Physic* (4th ed.).
Miller, Perry (1961), *The New England Mind: Vol. II, From Colony to Province*, Beacon Press, Boston.
Minogue, K. & Biddiss, M. (eds.) (1987), *Thatcherism*, Macmillan, London.
Mitchell, Alexander F. (1883), *The Westminster Assembly*, James Nisbet, London.
Mitchell, Alexander F. (1886), *Catechisms of the Second Reformation*, London.
Murray, Patricia (1980), *Margaret Thatcher*, W.H. Allen & Co., London.
Nichols, Josias (1596), *An Order of Household Instruction*.
Norton, John (1647), *A Brief and Excellent Treatise containing the Doctrine of Godliness*.
Nowell, Alexander (1570), *A Catechism, or First Instruction and Learning of Christian Religion*.
Nowell, Alexander (1577), *A Catechism, or Institution of Christian Religion*.
O'Neill, Onora (1981), 'Nozick's Entitlements' in Paul, J. (ed.), *Reading Nozick*, Blackwell, Oxford.
Paget, John (1601), *A Primer of Christian Religion*.
Palmer, Herbert (1644), *An Endeavour of Making the Principles of Christian Religion, namely the Creed, the Ten Commandments, the Lord's Prayer, and the Sacraments, plain and easy* (4th impression).
Parr, Elnathan (1614), *Ground of Divinity*.
Perkins, William (1608), *Works* (Vol. I), Cambridge.
Perkins, William (1609), *Works* (Vol. II and III), Cambridge.
Perkins, William (1617), *Works* (Vol. II), Cambridge.
Perkins, William (1970), *The Work of William Perkins*, ed. Breward, I., Courtenay Library of Reformation Classics 3, Appleford.
Preston, John (1636), *Four Godly and Learned Treatises* (4th ed.), London.
Preston, John (1641), *Sinnes Overthrow, or a Godly and Learned Treatise of Mortification* (4th ed.), London.
Price, J.L. (1974), *Culture and Society in the Dutch Republic during the Seventeenth Century*, Temple Smith, London.

Robertson, H.M., (1933), *Aspects of the Rise of Economic Individualism*, Cambridge University Press, Cambridge.

Rollock, Robert (1849), *Works*, Wodrow Society, Edinburgh.

Rutherford, Samuel (1655), *The Covenant of Life Opened*, Edinburgh.

Rutherford, Samuel (1885), *Quaint Sermons*, London.

Smith, Adam (1961), *The Wealth of Nations* (2 Vols.), Methuen, London.

Smith, Adam (1976), *The Theory of Moral Sentiments*, Oxford University Press, Oxford, reprinted by Liberty Classics, Indianapolis.

Spurr, J. (1991), *The Restoration Church of England*, Yale University Press, New Haven.

Steele, Richard (1684), *The Tradesman's Calling*.

Steele, Richard (1825), *The Husbandman's Calling*, Edinburgh.

Struther, W. (1628), *Christian Observations and Resolutions*, Edinburgh.

Tawney, R.H. (1926), *Religion and the Rise of Capitalism*, Penguin Books, Harmondsworth.

Taylor, Thomas (1653), *Works*.

Thatcher, Margaret (1977), *Let Our Children Grow Tall, Selected Speeches 1975-7*, Centre for Policy Studies, London.

Thatcher, Margaret (1989), *The Revival of Britain: Speeches on Home and European Affairs, 1975-88*, Aurum Press, London.

Thatcher, Margaret (1993), *The Downing Street Years*, Harper Collins, London.

Torrance, Thomas F. (1959), *The School of Faith: The Catechisms of the Reformed Church*, James Clarke & Co., London.

Tuckney, Anthony (1676), *Forty Sermons upon Several Occasions*, London.

Twisse, William (1633), *A Brief Catechetical Exposition of Christian Doctrine*.

Tyacke, Nicholas (1987), *Anti-Calvinists*, Clarendon Press, Oxford.

Ure, Andrew (1835), *Philosophy of Manufactures*, London.

Ussher, James (1645), *A Body of Divinity or the Sum and Substance of Christian Religion*, Downes & Bradger, London.

Ussher, James (1847), *Whole Works* (Vol. XI), Hodges & Smith, Dublin.

Vaux, Laurence, attrib., (n.d.), *Godly Contemplations for the Unlearned*.

Virell, Matthew (1594), *A Learned and Excellent Treatise containing all the principal grounds of Christian Religion*.

Warford, William, see Doulye, George.

Webbe, George (1612), *A Brief Exposition of the Principles of Christian Religion.*

Weber, Max (1930), *The Protestant Ethic and the Spirit of Capitalism*, George Allen & Unwin, London.

Weber, Max (1948), *From Max Weber: Essays in Sociology*, eds. Gerth, H.H. and Wright Mills, C., Routledge & Kegan Paul, London.

Weber, Max (1949), *The Methodology of the Social Sciences*, The Free Press, New York.

Weber, Max (1952), *Ancient Judaism*, The Free Press, New York.

Weber, Max (1958), *The City*, The Free Press, New York.

Weber, Max (1961), *General Economic History*, Collier Books, New York.

Weber, Max (1965-6), *The Sociology of Religion*, Social Science Paperbacks in association with Methuen & Co. Ltd., London.

Weber, Max (1978), 'Anticritical Last Word on *The Spirit of Capitalism*', *American Journal of Sociology*, 83, pp. 1105-31.

Weir, D.A. (1990), *The Origins of the Federal Theology in Sixteenth Century Reformation Thought*, Clarendon Press, Oxford.

Wenzel, Siegfried (1960 and 1967), *The Sin of Sloth: Acedia in Medieval Thought and Literature*, University of North Carolina Press, Chapel Hill.

Wesley, John (1825), *Sermons* (Vols. I and II), London.

White, Josias (1632), *A Plain and Familiar Exposition upon the Creed, X Commandments, Lord's Prayer and Sacraments* (7th ed.).

White, Peter (1992), *Predestination, Policy and Polemic*, Cambridge University Press, Cambridge.

Wilkinson, Henry (1629), *A Catechism* (3rd ed).

Wilson, Thomas (1620), *Saints by Calling, or Called to be Saints.*

Young, Hugo (1989), *One of Us*, Macmillan, London.

Young, H. and Sloman, A. (eds.) (1986), *The Thatcher Phenomenon*, BBC.

Index

Abernethy, John 45, 127
accidia, acedia 25
Albertus, Magnus 23
Ames, William 67, 68, 125, 130
Anglicanism 15
antinomianism 36, 125
Aquinas, *see* Thomas Aquinas
Arminius, Arminianism 14, 15, 16, 28, 124
  see also semi-Arminianism
Augsburg Confession of Faith 40
Augustine, St. 73
Austin, Samuel 77, 78, 130
avarice 24, 25, 26, 48, 50, 71
  and merchants 22
  see also covetousness

Ball, John 75, 76, 84
Baptists 62
Basil of Caeserea, St. 19
Baxter, Richard 9, 14, 16, 46, 54, 55, 57, 82, 83, 86, 88, 89, 105, 108, 111, 126
Bayley, Lewis 46, 51
Benedict, St., Benedictines 19, 20
Berthold of Regensburg 23, 24
Beruf 24, 31, 125
Beza, Theodore 33, 59, 65
Bromley of Sherriff-Hales, Lady 76
Bullinger, Henry 59

Caeserius of Heisterbach 21
calling, the 5, 6, 7, 9, 12, 23, 24, 30, 31, 33, 34, 35, 38, 39, 41, 42, 43,44, 45, 50, 52, 53, 55, 56, 62, 67, 68, 70, 71, 73, 80, 81, 82, 83, 84, 86, 87, 89, 92, 97, 98, 99, 108, 113, 126
  general and particular, defined 31–2
Calvin, John 5, 6, 15, 33, 34, 36, 38, 39, 46, 49, 57, 59, 64, 65, 66, 73, 88, 128
Calvinism, 6, 8, 13, 14, 15, 16, 31, 33, 39, 40, 44, 50, 52, 62, 100, 128
  in Scotland 27–8
  in Dutch Republic 28
Canisius, Peter 128
Carruthers, S.W. 61
Cartwright, Thomas 67
Cassian, John 19
Charles I 124
Church of England Prayer Book 59, 61, 67, 80
Church of Scotland 59, 60, 61, 66, 69, 95, 106
Cistercians 20, 21, 22
Clark, James 93, 94, 95
Cockburn, John 90
Colvill, William 46, 48, 57,127
confession 16, 24, 26, 39, 40, 126
consumerism 114

conversi 20
Cotton, John 53, 57
Council of Trent 128
covetousness 32, 48, 50, 57,
        66, 71, 72, 109
    see also avarice
Craig, John 66
Cranmer, Thomas 59, 67

Damian, Peter 25
Darien expedition 95
Davidson, Donald 14
deadly sins 24, 25
Defoe, Daniel 98, 99, 100
Denison, Stephen 81
Dering, Edward 81
Dickson, David 51, 89, 127
Dod, John and Cleaver,
        Richard 47, 49, 56, 127
Dominicans 21, 22, 23
Durham, James 48, 49, 52, 53,
        54, 127, 128
Dutch Reformed Church 15
Dutch Republic 27, 28, 29

Erasmus, Desiderius 129
Evagrius Ponticus 25

fall of man 18, 22, 35
Flavell, John 91, 94, 130
Franciscans 21, 22, 23
Franck, Sebastian 18
Franklin, Benjamin 4, 96, 97,
        98, 99, 100
Friedman, Milton 110, 131
Froude, J.A. 28, 84, 103

Gataker, Thomas 69
gifts, 57, 87, 88, 89
Glasgow 115–19
Good, William 69, 129
Goodwin, John 124

Gouge, William 69, 70
Gray, Andrew 51
Green, Ian 59
Greenham, Richard 76, 87, 127
Gregory the Great 25
Griffiths, Brian 109, 110, 111,
        131
Gunn, Neil 61

Hall Joseph 124
Hamilton, Archbishop (of St
        Andrews) 128
Hayek, Friedrich 103, 110,
        111, 131
Heidelberg Catechism 66
Hill, Christopher 17
Honorius of Autun 22
Hutcheson, George 46, 47, 127,
        130
Hyma, Albert 27, 28

ideal types 3, 33, 42, 125
indulgences 17
Industrial Revolution 1, 2, 9,
        11, 28, 60
investment ethic 86, 87, 90, 93

Janeway, James 91, 92
Japan 112, 113, 132
John of Salisbury 25
Joseph, Keith 111, 131
Judaism 12, 13
Judas 34
just price 52, 53

Keayne, Robert 53
Knappen, M.M. 53
Knox, John 62, 125, 126
Kolde, Dietrich 128

Larger Catechism 60, 84
Laud, Archbishop 76

Locke, John 89, 90
Luther, Martin 5, 30, 34, 35,
      36, 38, 39, 40, 59, 64, 65,
      66, 73, 126

MacAlister, Sir Donald 60, 61
McBey, James 61
MacGeorge, Andrew 115, 116,
      132
McUre, John 116
Marx, marxism 9, 29, 43, 44,
      105
Melville, Andrew 115
Methodism 14, 62, 107, 108,
      109, 131
Mico, John 77, 78
Mitchell, Alexander 69, 72, 73,
      74, 76, 129
Modern Western Capitalism 2,
      3, 10
Monasticism 13, 17, 18 f., 30,
      124

New Catechism 66
New England 53, 62
Newcomen, Matthew 74, 129
Nichols, Martin 74, 75, 76, 84,
      129
Nowell, Alexander 61, 67, 128

O'Neill, Onora 90, 130

Paget, John 81, 82, 83, 109,
      130
Palmer, Herbert 69, 70, 71, 72
Paterson, William 95, 130
Perkins, William 31, 32, 35,
      36, 38, 39, 40, 45, 46, 48,
      49, 51, 55, 67, 87, 130
predestination 5, 14, 15, 16, 34
Preston, John 47, 51, 87, 127
profit ethic 7, 8, 9, 10, 18, 26,
      29, 42–58, 63, 68, 96, 98,
      101, 104
      see also Protestant ethic,
      secondary
Protestant ethic 2, 4 ff., 7, 8, 9,
      10, 15, 16, 17, 18, 23, 24,
      68, 79, 84, 91, 104, 107,
      116
      primary 9, 24, Ch. 3, 55, 80,
      91, 94, 98
      see also work ethic
      secondary 9, Ch. 4
      see also profit ethic
Proverbs, Book of 19, 44, 51,
      93, 96, 98, 99, 126
purgatory 17
Puritanism 6, 14, 15, 32, 33,
      44, 52, 53, 56, 73, 79,
      102, 113
      English 29

Quakers 14

Rice-Davies, Mandy 44, 126
Roberts, Alfred 107, 112
Robertson, H.M. 39, 125, 126
Rogers, Ezekiel 78
Rollock, Robert 32, 47, 125
Roman Catholicism 12, 16, 17
Rutherford, Samuel 51, 56, 69,
      70, 129

sabbatarianism 107, 112
sanctification 37, 62
Scotland 27, 28, 29, 100, 104,
      125
Scottish Confession of Faith 37
Second Table of the Decalogue
      63, 76:
      see also Ten
      Commandments
Semi-Arminianism 16

Sermon on the Mound 106, 108, 109, 111, 131
Shorter Catechism 60, 61, 62, 63, 64, 68, 69, 70, 72, 73, 74, 75, 82, 83, 84, 91
sloth, slothfulness 24, 25, 31, 47, 98
Smiles, Samuel 104
Smith, Adam 54, 100, 101, 102, 103, 105, 110, 111, 131
solifideism 5, 35
spirit of capitalism 2, 7, 8, 9, 10, 17, 62, 63, 84, 87, 91, 96, 98, 103, 116
defined 3–4
see also profit ethic
Steele, Richard 92, 93, 94, 99, 127
stewardship 54, 55, 56, 57, 83, 86, 93, 109, 110, 111, 112, 127, 131
Struther, William 88

talents 83, 87, 88, 89, 93, 95, 106, 131
Parable of the 23
Tawney, R.H. 92, 93
Ten Commandments 30, 56, 62, 76
Thatcher, Thatcherism 106, 107, 108, 109, 110, 111, 112, 131
Thirty-Nine Articles 15
Thomas Aquinas 23, 125
Thomas of Chobham 22
Tuckney, Anthony 72, 127

Twisse, William 69, 70

Ure, Alexander 104
Ussher, James, Archbishop of Armagh 73, 74, 81, 83, 88, 129
usury 1, 22, 32, 71, 72

Vaux, Laurence 129
Venice 28, 29
Virell, Matthew 77, 78, 79, 80, 83

Walker, George 69
Warford, William 129
Webbe, George 78
Wenzel, Siegfried 25
welfare state 110, 111
Wesley, John 14, 108, 109, 110, 111, 131
Westminster Assembly of Divines 59–85
Westminster Confession of Faith 31, 73
Whatley, George 130
White, John 69, 70, 129
Wilkinson, Henry 69, 70, 72, 83
Wilson, Thomas 69, 70
work ethic 7, 9, 12, 18, 23, 26, 27–41, 49, 80, 108, 113, 131
see also Protestant ethic, primary

Yelverton, Sir Henry 124